Thriplow Time Trails

A Rough Archaeologist's Guide to an Ancient Village

Thriplow Landscape Research Group 2004

ACKNOWLEDGEMENTS

We have been very fortunate to obtain a grant from the Local Heritage Initiative, which is a partnership between the Heritage Lottery Fund, Nationwide Building Society and the Countryside Agency, and thank them, and William Wall from the Countryside Agency for their continued support. All the people we have asked for help have enthusiastically put themselves out to assist us. We would particularly like to thank the following experts for their helpful discussions and practical support.

Margaret Bennets
Yvonne Bird
Steve Boreham
Michelle Bullivant
The late Tony Carter
Graham Clark
Aileen Connor
Peter Cott
Carol Fletcher
Colin Forbes
Terry Hoare
Nicholas James
Steven Kemp
Thalia Liokatis
Chris Montague
Richard Mortimer

Sue Oosthuizen
Bob Randall
Colin Shell
Peter Speak
Peter Spufford
Alison Taylor
Christopher Taylor
David Trump
Dawn Veal
Twigs Way
Sharon Webb

We also thank the following people for giving their permission and encouragement.

Jim Mynors
Leslie Harrison
Nigel and Elizabeth Moore
Robert Smith
Amanda Tuck
Oliver Walston
Alan White

Finally we thank all those others who have contributed in so many different ways, smoothing the path towards the publication of this book.

Local Heritage *initiative*

Heritage Lottery Fund

Nationwide

The Countryside Agency

FOREWORD

One of my great pleasures, when I can find time amongst all my ongoing commitments, is to retreat to the peace and quiet of my cottage in Thriplow. When I am there, I often walk or cycle around the village and the surrounding countryside.

I have always had a fascination for the history of places and have noticed how different this quintessentially English village is from the stone buildings of my Yorkshire childhood. I have also noticed that the roads approaching the village are straight as a ruler, but the streets within the village are quite winding. Every village in the country has one or two of these idiosyncrasies that provokes you to think "I wonder why that is like it is?".

This book is the story of one group that finally said "We'll try to find out why". It shows what a dedicated team of enthusiasts can do with the backing of the Local Heritage Initiative and may even inspire others to write similar books about their villages.

The Right Honourable Baroness Boothroyd PC.

Photo: Lichfield

INTRODUCTION

This modest book is the result of several years of effort (and some false starts) by a disparate group of amateur landscape archaeologists who first met at a course on Landscape Archaeology in 1998 with Dr Nicolas James.

At the end of the course, rather than disperse to go our separate ways we decided to hold informal meetings to discuss how we could apply the knowledge gained from Dr James' interesting ideas. We decided that we should apply our new skills on a South Cambridgeshire village, and after much discussion chose Thriplow as it had a somewhat atypical shape and no obvious centre. We were especially intrigued by its having what appeared to be a *"ring road"*. This is OK for large towns but Thriplow?

We set ourselves the task of answering the question "Why is Thriplow in its present shape?" After much agonising and as the result of carrying out a number of walks along the footpaths (trails) in and around Thriplow, and the surveying of some sites indicating past man made activity, we began to think that we may be able to provide some answers to this intriguing question.

Rather than restrict these ideas to what may be considered "pure" archaeology we have decided to extend our presentation to other aspects taking in geology, botany/natural history, surveying techniques, architecture and even what may be considered "fringe" topics such as leylines. These aspects are very much interrelated so it seemed sensible to deal holistically with the landscape archaeology and history of Thriplow. Having the luxury of amateur status left us free from the constraints of professional activities to focus on what WE thought was of interest, hence the somewhat eclectic range of topics covered in this book. This diverse range of topics is only part of the story, the thread binding them together is the story of a group of individuals working together, learning new skills and trying them out in the context of this particular village.

The main part of the book comprises 9 "trails" or "Time Trails" and you are invited to wander along these observing and enjoying the various aspects of archaeology, geology, environment and nature. We should warn you that some of these trails can be quite muddy, especially after rain so DO use suitable footwear or even wellies (but these do not need to be green!). Having taken care to ensure that these trails are on recognised footpaths we do urge you not to wander off these onto private property!

We have tried to make the text flow, from trail to trail, by describing the story of the people in the group, hopefully producing an interesting but not too stodgy narrative, but only you the reader can judge how well we have succeeded in that! Scattered throughout the text are boxes, which give a little background with plenty of illustrations if you can't find the time to wander the village itself. We have included appendixes for some more detailed discussion and description of many of the topics mentioned in the main part of the book, contents on page 85. We welcome any comments, especially on some of the more controversial items

www.thriplowlandscape.cambscommunitygroups.org.uk.

This is a book for everyone, everywhere, showing how you can look into the origins of your home. Don't accept that THE book of your area has been written, or that there is nothing more to discover. If there is a book - all it represents is the view of the author, based on what has been discovered up to date! You do not have to dig holes in the ground to get going, just keep your eyes and your mind open.

Ask yourself why this road is straight but bumpy, why this field is a funny shape, or why the local street plan is particularly complex. If you cannot answer the question - there is something left for you to discover. No town or village in the United Kingdom, or anywhere else, has been fully understood or can fully answer the questions, why is this here and why is it like this? New discoveries are frequently unearthed even in London, and one of the best documented villages in the country, Landbeach in Cambridgeshire, could easily still have undiscovered remains within 500 yards of its church.

Photo Tony Jedrej.
Countryside Commission

Thriplow Landscape Research Group, from left:
Shirley Wittering, Ian Sanderson, Elizabeth Livingstone, Pat Davies, Jim Wilson, Bruce Milner, Brian Bridgland.

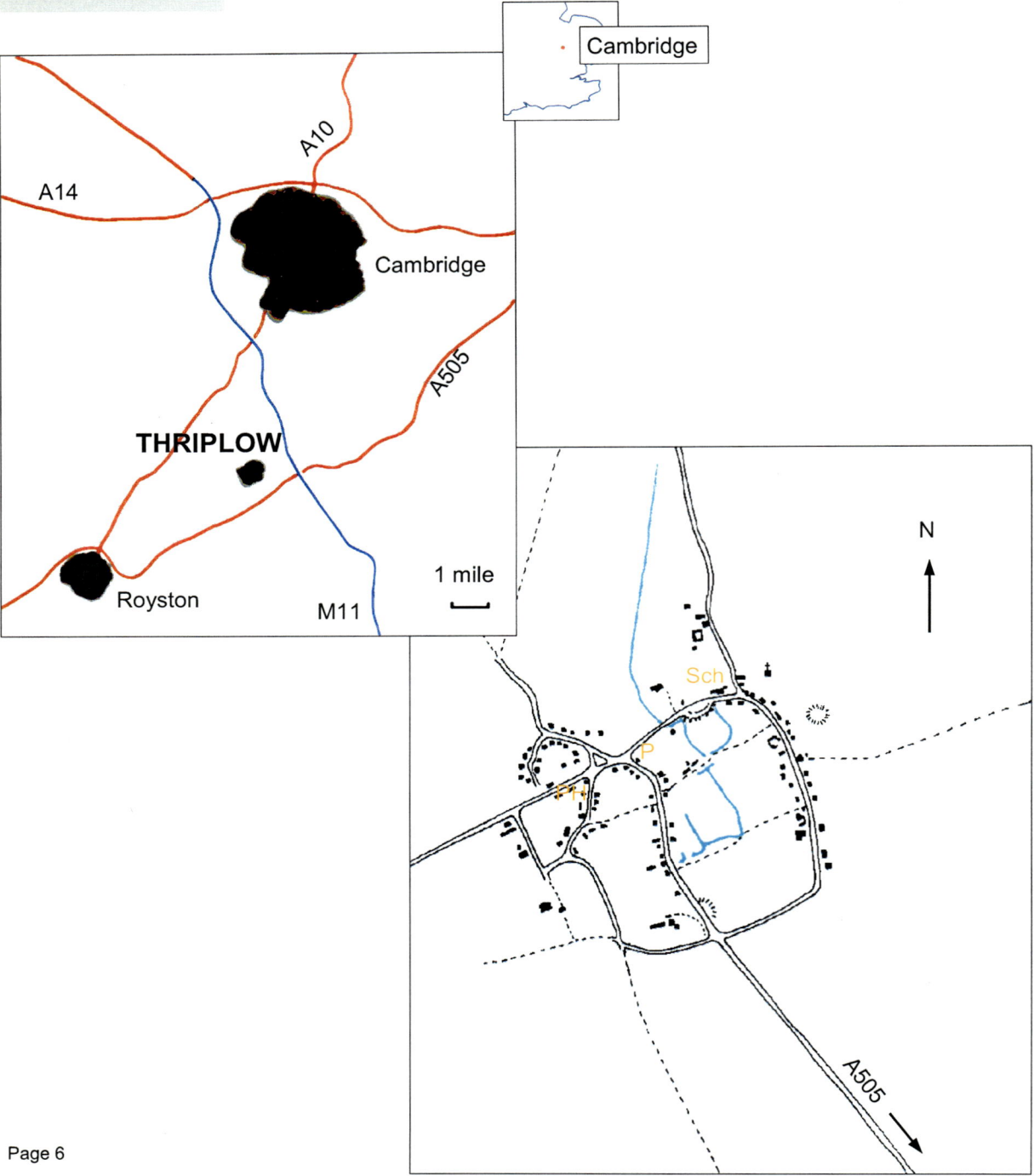

Thriplow Time Trails

Cambridge

A10

A14

Cambridge

A505

THRIPLOW

Royston

M11

1 mile

N

Sch

P

PH

A505

THRIPLOW IN CAMBRIDGESHIRE

The parish of Thriplow, situated on low chalk hills, is about 8 miles South West of Cambridge. The presence of springs and fertile land has supported farming for more than 3000 years. Having been bypassed by major roads and railways it has maintained an unspoilt character.

The village itself has a school, a pub and a church providing for a population of about 460. It is famous for its annual "Daffodil Weekend", which attracts craft stalls and tourists from a wide area.

On visiting the village, the most notable features are the compact village green with its whitewashed village smithy opposite the war memorial, or for nature lovers, the nature reserve noted for its orchids. It is accessible from the footpath marked in the field facing the modern village hall. Near the church are classic thatched cottages.

An examination of the map gives the impression of a "ring road" around the village. This is misleading as some is single-track road, which should be driven with caution as it is well protected with fierce speed bumps. The modern A505 in the South part of the parish follows one of the ancient trackways of the Icknield Way.

TRAIL 1
THRIPLOW MEADOWS

Enter Thriplow Meadows over the stile and notice the old oak trees. One old lady in the village remembers when this field, Godson's Grove, was once full of oak trees.

Go through the gate to enter the adjoining meadow where the most important plants are the marsh orchids.

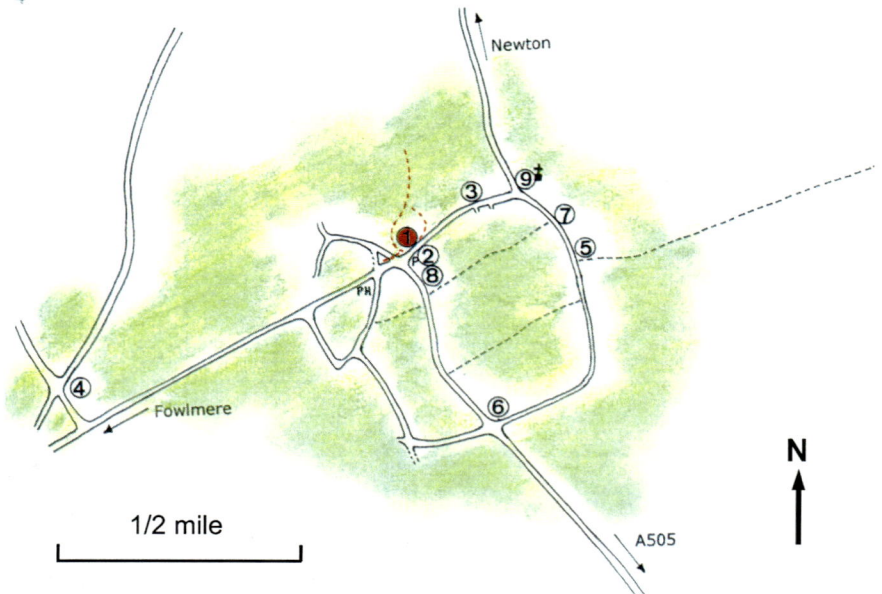

Newton

Fowlmere

1/2 mile

N

A505

The Southern Marsh Orchid *Dactylorhiza praetermissa* produces a spectacular display of cylindrical purple, red, and pink flower spikes at the end of June and the beginning of July. Closely related are the paler hued earlier flowering orchids, the Early Marsh Orchid *Dactylorhiza incarnata*. The bee orchid *Ophrys apifera*, so often found on Cambridgeshire chalklands, is found here only on the drier margins. In the late 1960s over 4000 orchids were counted in one meadow alone and it could be said that Thriplow had one of the largest surviving populations of marsh orchids in East Anglia.

Grazing animals are very important - horses and cows are selective grazers and the continual treading of the ground prevents the establishment of tree seedlings and the taller marsh grasses. Without cultivation but with regular grazing and with a high water-table in poorly drained soils, a closely cropped, floristically rich, open meadowland is created. Left alone in these conditions nature will ultimately produce mature oak woodland. To manage the meadows they are grazed or selectively mown.

Return through Thriplow Meadows.

Ealdorman Byrhtnoth, illustrated on the village sign, was killed at the battle of Maldon fighting the Danes in 991. He bequeathed his estates, which included Thriplow, to the Abbot of Ely.

This 18th Century smithy, maintained by the Thriplow Society, can be seen in action at the annual Daffodil Weekend each Spring.

Outside to put theory into practice…….

The thing that was missing from our classroom lectures on landscape archaeology was the outside. We'd seen photographs, pored over maps, read books telling you how to interpret the landscape, even handled the odd bit of flint and pottery; but it's not the same as the real thing. So, having decided that Thriplow merited our close study, we went to find some lumps and bumps to investigate in the village. A walk from the village green to the nature reserve quickly confirmed that there were definitely some strange shapes hidden in the first field and we celebrated our freedom from the classroom with a massive dose of speculation as to what might have caused them. Having got that out of our systems, the results of our training cut in and we addressed the first problem - where do you start?

This was easy in one sense but difficult in another. Easy to see whether somebody else had already written down what previously stood in the field. Difficult to find out where they might have written it down. This was the first, but far from the last, time that the advantages of the disparate skills and interests of individual members of our group became apparent. We searched for any relevant documents in the Cambridge Collection in the Central Library and in the County Records office at Shire Hall. One of our group even painstakingly translated the 'Thriplow Hundred Rolls' from Latin.

HISTORICAL SOURCES FOR THRIPLOW

Among the earliest historical documents for Thriplow are two books in Latin called *Liber Ramsiensis* and *Liber Eliensis*, both of which are copies of earlier texts.

The next document is the Domesday Book compiled in 1086 to enable King William I to classify his lands for tax purposes. There are three versions.

1279 another survey was made for the king; these are the Hundred Rolls or *Rotuli Hundredorum*. They are complete for Cambridgeshire and are far more detailed than Domesday, listing every single person in each parish.

From the sixteenth century it became law that all baptisms, marriages and burials should be recorded in a register by the clergy of each parish. These documents give an invaluable resource for family historians keen to trace their families back in time.

This 1537 script is translated on the following page.

In 1661 King Charles II was restored to the throne only to find his coffers empty. A means had to be found to raise some money fairly quickly and someone had the bright idea of taxing everyone's hearths. The village constable went round his village noting how many hearths each person had. The tax, a shilling a hearth, was collected twice a year until it was abolished in 1689. The window tax replaced it!

The Hearth Tax returns can be linked with wills and inventories of the same period to give a detailed picture of the number of rooms in peoples' houses and the furniture and belongings they possessed.

In 1801 the first nationwide census was taken by the government, first to gauge manpower resources during the Napoleonic wars and to settle disputes over whether the population was expanding or not. From 1841 the census lists all people, their place of origin, their occupation, age and position within the family and where they lived.

All these documents are kept in the County Record Office, at Shire Hall, Cambridge.

Photo: David Ward, Countryside Agency

All the documents gave snippets of historical information, some of which was useful, but a lot referenced places to other places that either no longer exist or may have been modified in the intervening years. *"Item; !$\frac{1}{2}$ acres in the same furlong between the demesne land of the Lord Bishop on the West and the land half on townsendeland on the east and abutting on Foulmerewaye on South and on land of the bondsmen of the Lord Bishop on North."* This translation of the 1537 script is a description of the whereabouts of one of the strips in the open fields of Thriplow.

A field bounded by a stream is another case in point, particularly when a number of the water courses in the village look to have been straightened up to the extent of having right angle bends - definitely not a natural water course. Who's to say the stream course wasn't just straightened but was relocated entirely, probably increasing the land holding of a local dignitary at the same time.

One very useful opportunity occurred whilst we were mulling over our collected documentary evidence. The Thriplow society had one of its monthly meetings on the history of the village, and people were invited to bring along anything they'd found of interest. Naturally we attended and pored over old photographs, listened to reminiscences and scrutinised odd bits of pottery, farm implements and intriguingly what looked like a bit of hypocaust tiling someone had dug up in their garden.

Further research continued at home.

Map of Thriplow showing surface water in 1840.

The lighter blue indicates flowing water and darker blue shows standing water.

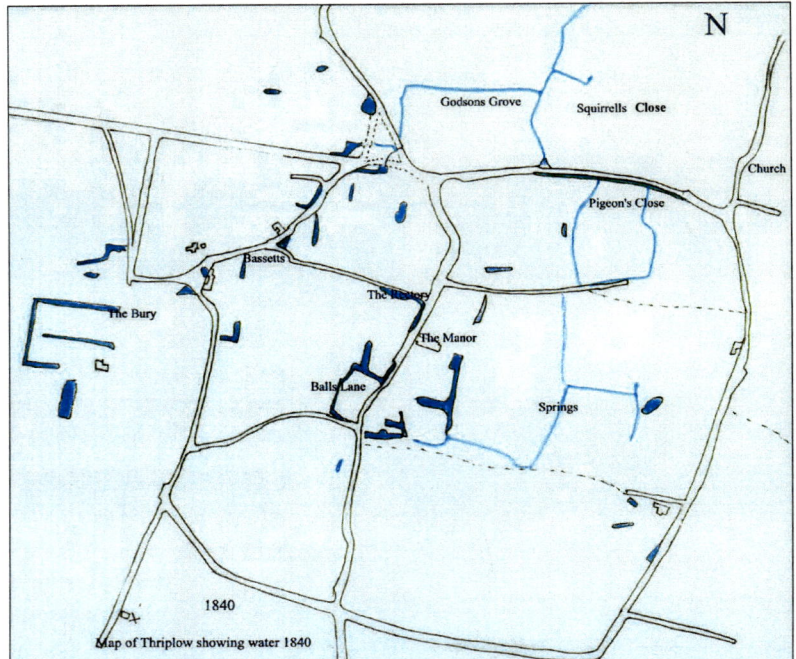

Map of Thriplow showing water 1840

WHITHER THRIPLOW IN 1310?

A rather intriguing statistic which perhaps has not been fully explained is the apparent drop in the population of Thriplow between 1279 as obtained by the Hundred Rolls and that estimated from the Lay Subsidy of 1327. At the earlier date a population of 430 was recorded while 48 years later we only have an estimated 150.

Why this apparently enormous population drop?
It was NOT due to the Black Death as that started in 1349 but was more likely a result of the extremely wet and cold weather in the 1310s. It is thought that this had a particularly severe effect on the population of Thriplow as there is evidence that there was a settlement on the lower ground to the west of the church. Imagine being cold and hungry in a mud hut then having to contend with a permanently soggy floor as well!

We believe that this is the reason there are now longer any pre 18th century buildings in this part of Thriplow. The only remnants are the indications of a moat near the school field and the hollow-way in the field some 200m to the west. And the name of the road - Gutter Lane!

The trees did not like the weather at this time either, from the evidence provided by tree ring data which showed the slowest tree growth between 1300 – 1320.
This can be seen in the diagram opposite.
More details are in the appendix.

Differences in tree ring width between 1200 and 1400 A.D.

tree ring width (mm)

Years,(5 yearly average)

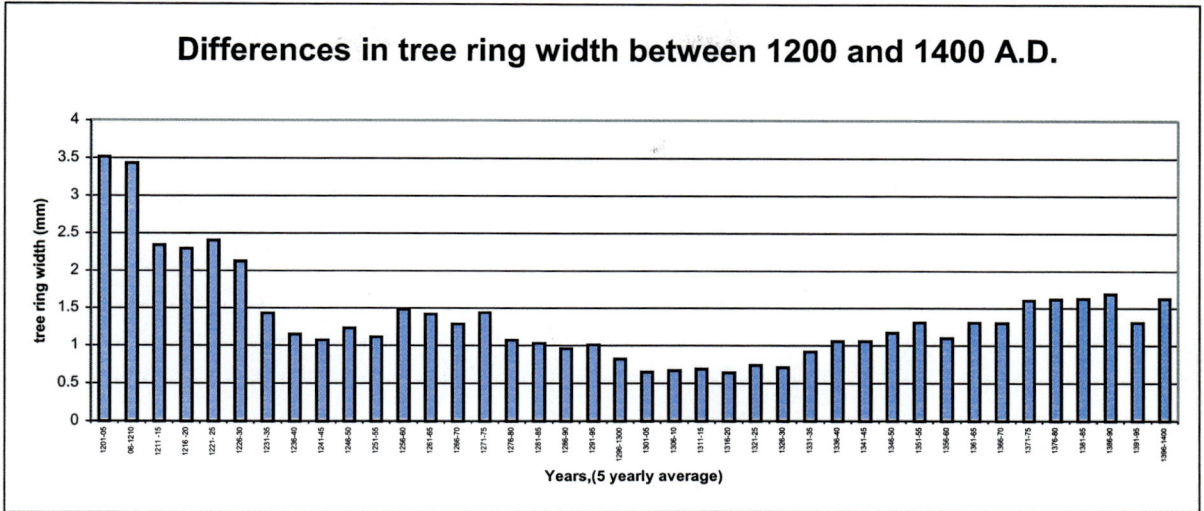

Our intrepid group finally started its on the ground investigation of the field on a cold autumn Sunday morning. We had sought the advice of the local Archaelogical Field Unit (A.F.U.) on how a group of beginners should go about this task, and they had explained that to make some sense of a field of lumps and bumps, it first needed to be surveyed. That seemed sensible, we had said, but how do we do it with no equipment and even if we had, not a clue on how to work a theodolite or whatever. No problem said the A.F.U., one of our archaeologists has volunteered to give up his Sunday morning to get you started.

Steve Kemp duly turned out on the appointed day and using a wooden plane table on a wooden tripod and a sighting device, all of which seemed to have 'War Department' markings on, helped us produce our first site survey.

We were proud of our survey, despite its slightly battered appearance, and fascinated by the way it evolved before our eyes like a very slow join the dots drawing.

The basic technique was actually very simple once you got the hang of it, but fraught with difficulty in the detail!

The first catch is one that we still have trouble with now. We were using a 'plane' table as our drawing board. 'Plane' in this context means flat. Flat means level, forward and back, and side to side, checked with a spirit level both ways and adjusted by altering the stand. Unfortunately with three legs it seems to require a definite knack to keep the level one way whilst finding it the other way.

There were other problems too, even a simple job such as holding the sighting pole vertical becomes difficult when you get cold.

Measuring the distances should have been easy, but with large plants in the way and having to juggle around the tripod legs our progress was slower than expected. Even the height of the drawing board was troublesome for the shorter members who were on tip toe in their wellies whilst the taller members had to crank themselves down!

One particular hazard to field surveying happens when a cow wanders across your line of sight. Rapid discussion ensues to identify a volunteer to make herding gestures and move the blockage along, much to the amusement and relief of the rest!

HOW TO MAKE A PLANE TABLE SURVEY

Plane Table surveying is the most basic and reasonably accurate way of making a map of an area. The only specialist equipment you need is a flat board, a sighting device and a tape measure. The technique is easy to master and has the advantage that you can see your map developing as you go on.

1. Set up your board on a stand.
2. Place the sighting device on the board and line it up so that one edge is on the mark indicating where the board is located.
3. Then line up the sight with the target object.
4. Measure the distance to the target with a tape.
5. Calculate what that distance is according to your map scale.
6. Measure that length along the edge of the sight and make a mark. This fixes both the distance and direction of the target from the reference point (where the board is set up).
7. Repeat for all the target objects. These can be fence posts, trees, dips or bumps in the ground, or anything that you want to record.

Someone holding a pole on the relevant point makes it easy to locate non-vertical features such as bumps or dips.

There were further unexpected difficulties when we retired to the pub for lunch. We found that fixed things, like a water trough, seemed to have ambled about 10m South during the process! Tricky. We couldn't figure it out until we spotted some evidence of fresh disruption around the trough and eventually concluded that the farmer had appeared whilst we were away, and moved the trough to make it easier to get his vehicle through! A lesson well learned – make sure your fixed points are fixed!

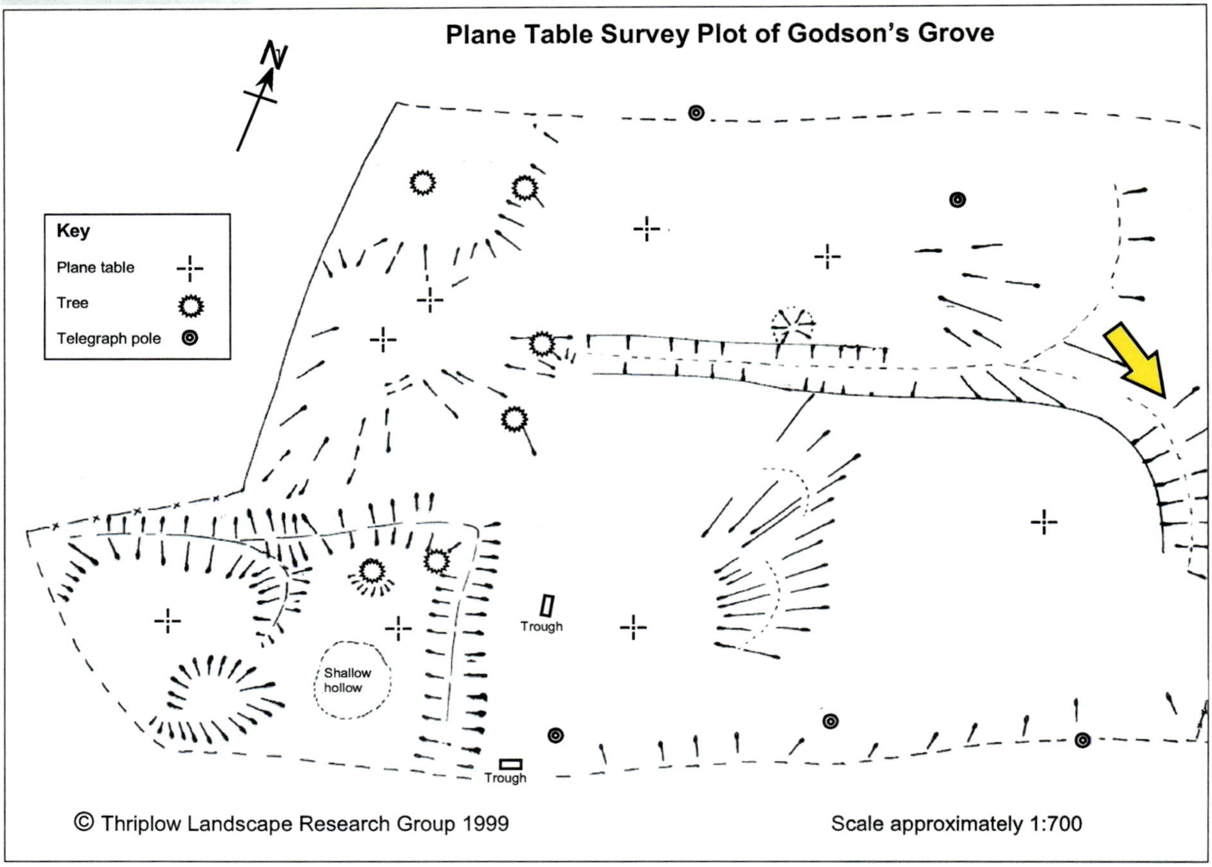

Plane Table Survey Plot of Godson's Grove

Key

Plane table	-‡-
Tree	✿
Telegraph pole	◉

Trough

Shallow hollow

Trough

© Thriplow Landscape Research Group 1999

Scale approximately 1:700

This picture shows the curve of one of the ditches as indicated by the yellow arrow on the plan.
It is easy to see the shape of the ditches during the winter when the pattern is marked out by changes in the colour of the vegetation. Grass at the bottom of these depressions is a brighter green, bordered by tussocks of light brown dried grass.

HOW TO READ A PLOT

Hachures are symbols that show the positions of the top and bottom of a slope.

Thinner and more widely spaced hachures of a more gentle slope........

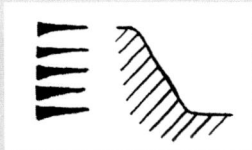

Those in the plot opposite have rounded heads as the changes in slopes that they mark are very gradual.
If there were sharp changes the hachures would look more like those below. The wide end represents the top and the narrow end the bottom.

A rounded mound.......

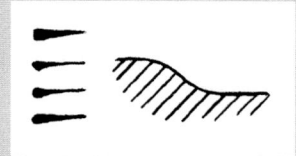

These are the thicker, flat headed and closely spaced hachures of a steep slope.......

A steeply cut pit.........

We used this plane table technique to produce our survey shown opposite. The aim was to try and resolve the problem of whether a particularly bumpy bit of the field was in fact a platform indicating that there used to be a house in the SW corner.

Standing in the field it was very difficult to make sense of the lumps and bumps, but once we had produced the map it suggested that there might be a house platform. This platform appeared to have a clear boundary to the field running roughly NS and EW. It seems that the platform had later been cut away, probably to provide watering points or access, or possibly just to get some clunch for road surfacing.

TRAIL 2
WASH PIT

The Red Lion pub once stood where there is now a smart new village hall. During W.W.2 the Red Lion was burnt down. Then the American Air Force presented the village with a chicken shed which was converted into a village hall. This was replaced in 2000 when the new village hall was built.

Start by the village hall and turn East along School Lane. There are often cattle grazing in the field to your left.

Newton

PH

Fowlmere

N

A505

1/2 mile

School Lane was once aptly called Gutter Lane, following the line of the stream. The stream was slightly wider at this point to allow sheep to be dipped before clipping.

School Lane crosses a small stream near the electricity sub station. There is a bench mark indicated on the map here....but it's not easy to find.

Before you reach the school pause to look over the fence where there are often horses. Speculate about why the ditch in this meadow is curved and then read further to see what we thought about this.

A groma. You are not likely to see one now but they may have been used here in the past. Read later to find out.

Interestingly, where the school now stands was once called Savages Close. The school was built in 1864 as a rival to the Non-Conformist school in Fowlmere Road.

The Village Hall carpark was a familiar meeting place for our group but we had been seen and collared to present our activities to a meeting of the Thriplow Society. One cold winter evening the three presenters and some supporters from our group entered the new village hall and after some adjustments with cables and projectors we told our story to a number of interested villagers.

Much less successful than our talk to the Thriplow Society meeting was our search, a few months later, for bench marks in the village on the stretch of road between the pub and the school. We needed these to try and determine the relative heights of the bits of surveying we'd done at various times.

We'd studied the maps and could fairly well, to within a few yards, determine where a height marker should be. They weren't there! There was a bench mark on the wall of the pub and one on the wall of the school but of the three heights marked in between on the current map – not a sign. We finally decided that two may have been covered up when the road was re-surfaced, but the other one which is listed as a bench mark, eludes us to this day.

The one at the school is interesting in that it is new, being re-carved into the brickwork when the old Victorian one was covered up by an extension - makes you wonder who thinks of these little details!

Bench mark re-carved into the school wall.

We have spent many hours investigating a field at the back of the school. This field is a gently rising, fairly innocuous paddock, but, as we discovered when we clambered over the gate and sank gently into the mud, it contains a whole variety of interesting lumps and bumps.

The two most interesting features, for a landscape archaeologist, are the distinctly soft muddy area near to the gate and a ditch with a right angle bend roughly following the school fence. There is also a spring and an old chalk quarry towards the other edge of the field.

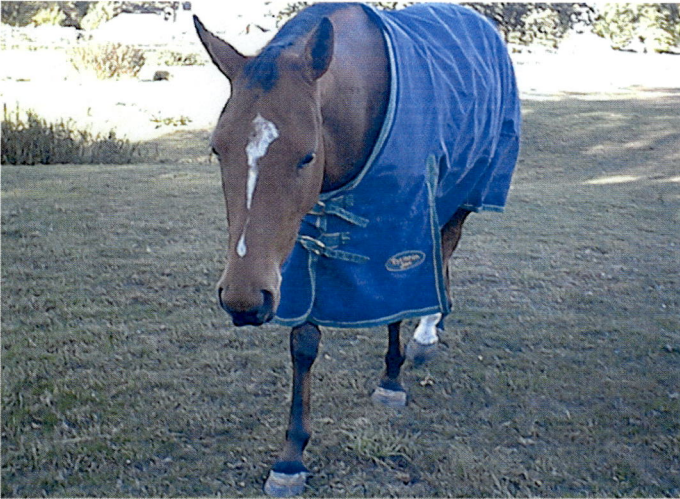

"Paddocks are by and large inhabited by horses."

These features can be seen clearly from the top of the church tower, especially when there is bright evening sunshine as there was when we climbed up.

On our first visit to the field, after recovering the odd wellington boot stuck in the mud, we wandered about speculating wildly about the size and shape of the ditch, matching moats around manors and finally deciding that we needed to investigate this some more. We'd just finished our first exercises in plane table surveying, so this seemed like the ideal opportunity to try out those skills on our own.

The day arrived, fine and brisk. The owner was happy, so we heaved the surveying gear from the cars to the field. We carefully followed our lessons and surveyed the field, stretching tapes from the table to the fence and wherever seemed appropriate.

Paddocks are, by and large, inhabited by horses. This one was. We were slowly becoming aware that animals in fields generally like a bit of quiet interest but can miss some of the finer points of the surveyor's art, such as tape measures or lines of sight, or carefully adjusted tripods. Sometimes they seem to enjoy an audience to show how fast they can gallop or jig about, not unlike having half a ton of three year old helping! One of our number was despatched to mediate.

More intimidating was the horse and rider emerging through the school gate and over the school playing field to check that we weren't surveying for a new supermarket or park and ride. One of our number was despatched to soothe.

View of the school
looking down from the
church tower.

The map we produced was messy. What had seemed straight forward when there was someone there to ask, suddenly became full of pitfalls and errors. We were all impressed though when we saw the messy map transformed by inking in the relevant detail and erasing the crossings out.

This gave rise to a renewed bout of speculation when we compared the distances with other moated sites and found that the shape was about the right size for a moated site. We called in the experts for our next contemplation of the site.

Steve Kemp spent some of a Sunday afternoon offering his thoughts on this particular site but even with the support of another professional archaeologist passing on her bicycle, they failed to make a dent in our wild speculations. The question was, what to do next?

We decided to find out more about the ditch by augering. Not peering over steaming entrails in search of inspiration, more laboriously drilling a hole in the ground.

Our helpful archaeologist duly turned up on yet another weekend with a pile of metalwork which needed carting from the cars to the site. He explained how the bits fitted together, and regretted that he couldn't demonstrate because of his bad back. We soon realised how he'd got a bad back.

This technique involves persuading an inch diameter metal tube to penetrate about 3 feet into the ground, pulling it out and looking at the soil that has been forced into the inside of the tube. It's not all bad, the tube has a pointed end!

Luckily the soil was in good condition, not too wet and not too dry and, better than that, not too stony. It took only a few minutes though before our two stalwart volunteers had discarded all their outer coverings whilst the rest stood around huddled against a cold breeze and wishing for an extra layer.

The soil in the tube finally emerged and was carefully cleaned up with an old kitchen knife, leaving a tube of soil shaded in different ways down to a bottom half inch of chalk, where our soil corers had finally admitted defeat.

It was at this point that we fully appreciated the verbal skills of the wine tasters describing raspberry notes and piquancy in fine wines basically translating a taste into words. Soils at this point seemed to have a similar translation problem. Yes, the white bit at the bottom was chalk and the bit at the top was slightly darker brown with slightly more bits of stone followed by a still slightly darker layer.

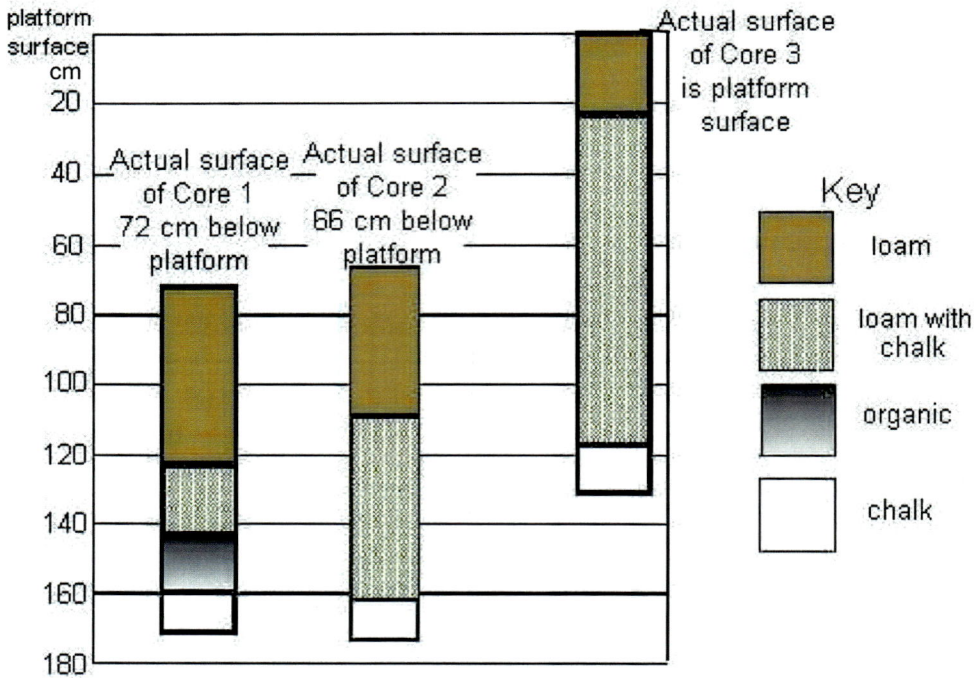

platform surface cm

20 — 40 — 60 — 80 — 100 — 120 — 140 — 160 — 180

Actual surface of Core 1 72 cm below platform

Actual surface of Core 2 66 cm below platform

Actual surface of Core 3 is platform surface

Key

loam

loam with chalk

organic

chalk

We did our best, and there were distinct boundaries in the recovered mud, carefully measured off.

The most exciting was a thin band of particularly dark soil near the bottom of some samples which we were told was a humus or peaty layer where vegetation had rotted in the ditch before soil had gathered on top.

This showed that the ditch had been kept open sometime in the past long enough for vegetation to grow around and rot into the ditch. When we compared the depths at which we found chalk, it also showed that about half a metre of chalk had been removed in making the ditch.

We were stuck as to where to go next, having lost the necessary energy for augering, and the equipment had to go back anyway, but we'd been watching Time Team so we thought that a bit of geophysics might clarify the situation.

We'd heard of a gentleman who had the necessary kit for a resistivity survey so we asked him to help. Peter Cott came to help us. After looking over the site he suggested that the school playing field would be a good place to start as this might show us whether the ditch had been covered up when the playing field had been levelled.

Having taken the precaution of obtaining permission from the head teacher in advance there was no hesitation in setting out a grid and ambling about the playing field with our magic zimmer frame. This most conveniently needs three people, one to drive the frame along, one to hold the cable so it doesn't get tangled up and one to help move the guide rope to keep the driver on line.

"GEOFIZZ"

Remember Channel Four's Time Team with Tony Robinson aka Baldrick and the frequent use of "geofizz" to map out where the buried wall foundation might be?. This refers to the use of geophysical techniques which can explore underneath the soil for man made disturbances or artefacts without having to dig into the ground. The most commonly used "geofizz" techniques are **soil resistivity, soil magnetometry and metal detecting.** Of these, metal detecting is, of course, specific for the detection of metallic objects buried under the soil.

Magnetic techniques measure variations in magnetic properties of the soil, which are significant in regions subjected to heat such as fires, ovens and kilns.

The Thriplow Landscape Research Group has recently bought a resistance measurement system from the C.I.A. (the Council for Independent Archaeology actually, not the other one!) It is a TRCIA 2 probe 50 cm device with image processing software.

Remnants of walls, tracks, graves etc buried 0.5 – 1m may often give a detectable imprint as a consequence of the differences in their ability to conduct electricity. To put it another way, by how much they resist an electric current relative to the surrounding undisturbed soil.

The diagram gives an idea of how the hidden evidence of man's activity can be revealed from a carefully conducted survey.

More details are in the appendix.

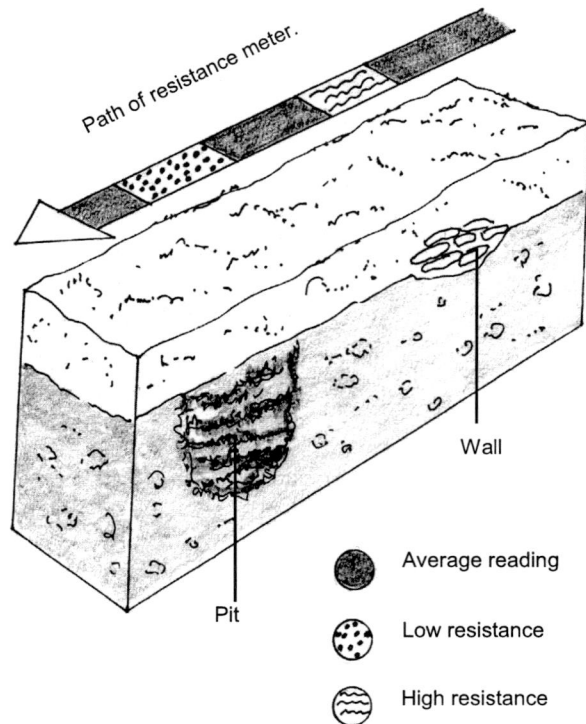

Path of resistance meter.

Wall

Pit

Average reading

Low resistance

High resistance

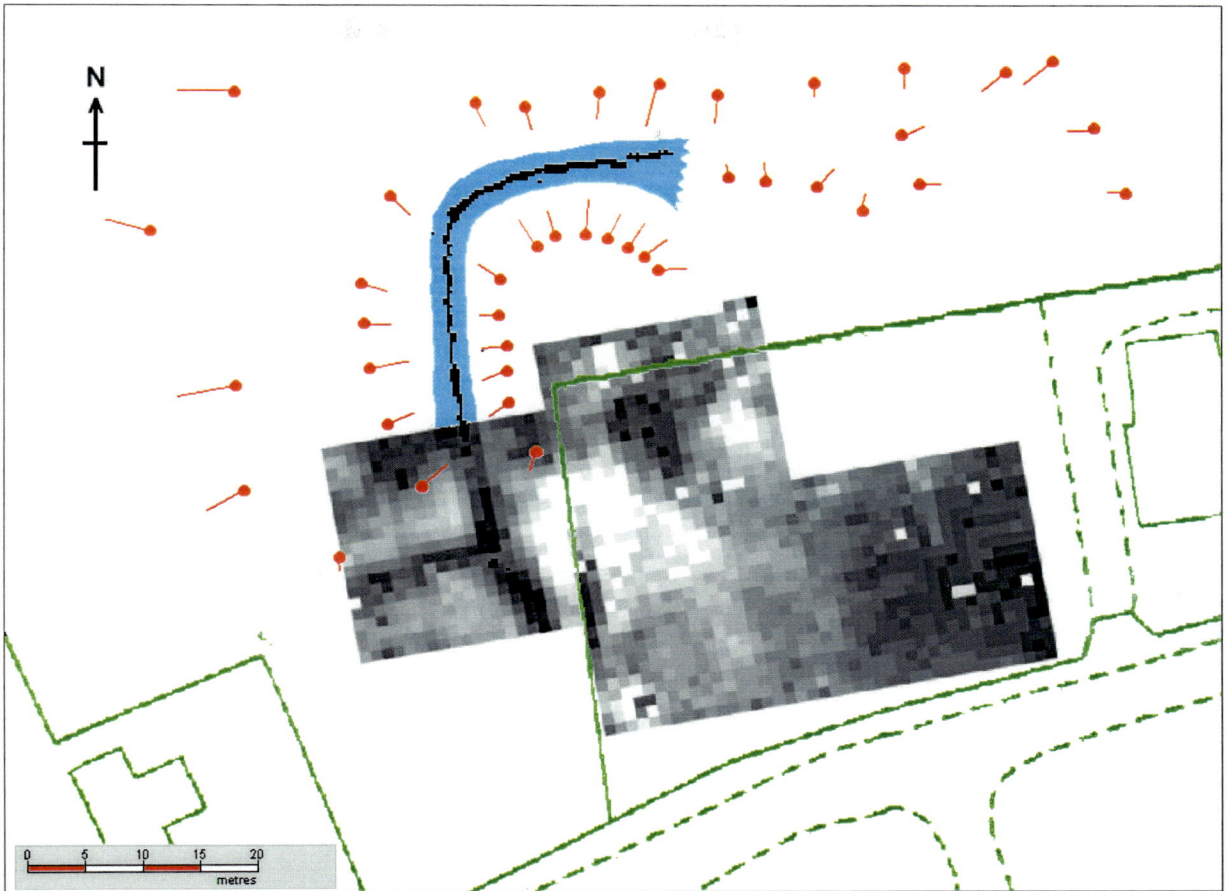

The diagram shows how all the pieces of surveying come together. The green outline shows the position of the school and the road outside, the red pin-like hachures show how the ground slopes in to a right angle ditch, (the lowest points highlighted in blue). The black, grey and white small squares in larger blocks (grids) show how the soil resistance varied at various points. In this diagram light areas denote high resistance and dark indicates low resistance.

These show that the ditch continues for about another 10m then splits in two directions. It also shows that diagonally across the school playing field, something is causing a very marked change in resistance. This could be a distinct oval area if you extend the lines of the hatchings.

In the bottom left of the school playing field, the shape of the children's sandpit can be clearly seen. Resistivity changes don't always indicate archaeology!

Because of this high tech innovation we'd got a full turnout of our group, which left four of us hanging about with nothing to do. It's at moments like these that the strangest ideas come out and the one of the moment was dowsing.

We had all heard about dowsing, and we all knew that 'proper' archaeologists assign it to the 'crank' category. We also knew that if you get a 'proper' archaeologist on their own, they sometimes admit to trying dowsing if they've run out of ideas or resources and no one is looking!

With no professional reputation to tarnish, we rapidly came up with some bent coat hangers and criss-crossed over the field, carefully planting markers when the wires swung together. Quite a plausible pattern of a building gradually emerged on the ground, but all we could do was record it on our plan whilst we waited for the true technology of resistance measurement to catch up.

Unfortunately this had hit problems in weaving in and out the school fence to extend the recording area. Ultimately the electronics decided enough was enough and quietly died. As we were packing up one of our number briefly thought he was joining the electronics as he inadvertently experimented with metal poles and the electrified horse fence.

Luckily the data we'd already gathered was retrieved and showed an interesting strong line across the site. Yet another item to look at in the future

DOWSING

Dowsing or divining or even witching, as it is sometimes known, has had a long history. The idea of being able to 'see' what is hidden below ground is a very powerful one. Archaeologists of course are very interested in discovering hidden structures and artefacts and dowsing was used (and in some cases still is) by such local experts as T.C.Lethbridge who was the Cambridge Antiquarian Societies Director of Excavations for 30 years. He used a pendulum, which purported to change direction of swing when over an archaeological feature.

Our group was interested in the idea of dowsing and wanted to see if it was possible to use the technique in our field investigations in Thriplow. Although the traditional picture of dowsing involves a Y shaped hazel twig held at arms length which jerks when over a hidden object or water, we used a much more prosaic method of two lengths of bent metal wire (actually from a metal coat hanger!) held in each hand. The idea was that the wires would cross over when activated by the hidden object. The mechanism of how this could happen is of course a mystery.

A series of recent scientific experiments has shown that no discernible physical effects are taking place. However, those who practise dowsing say they 'feel' the presence of the object or feature that they are looking for. In our case we set up a test grid on an area that we suspected contained an Iron Age hearth. Several people tried the technique and most found the metal wire move by crossing over itself. However, an analysis of the positions showed no obvious pattern at all. The conclusion must be that we were either not 'tuned in' correctly or that there is no interaction between the dowser and the obscured object. No doubt the debate will continue!

So did all this surveying, augering and dowsing indicate the site of a moated manor house perhaps similar to that at the nearby village of Pampisford?

Even if we don't yet know, we learned a lot about how to use these skills.

It was about this point that we realised that we'd been getting an enormous amount of help from a variety of people, taking up their weekends, borrowing equipment and generally imposing. It was also about that time that the Countryside Agency Local Heritage Initiative was being publicised. We put two and two together and put in a bid for some equipment, some funds for training, and some funds for a publication of our exploits.

William Wall from the Countryside Agency guided us through the process of form filling with great patience, and continued to provide help and advice even after the relevant committee agreed that our bid was in order.

First on the agenda was the business of levels. We'd got the hang of producing a map of a site, but not of recording how much it went up and down other than in general terms. Sunday morning arrived, as did our trainer with a dumpy level. Why it was 'dumpy' escaped us, but after wandering about the area for 3 hours we'd learnt the exact height of the school doorstep and along the way struggled to take in backsights and foresights and the various calculations needed. Much to our surprise, and credit to our trainer, we even managed to use the technique when we used our funding to purchase a theodolite.

A dumpy level is basically a telescope on a base that rotates. It enables you to read heights off a distant vertical measure. A theodolite is a dumpy level where the telescope also tilts up and down. Professionals use a Total Station which is a theodolite with computer interface and recording.

The residents of Thriplow must have been amazed when our wondrous new tool was finally delivered. Unable to wait for the weekend, we gathered in the village hall car park just after dusk had fallen on an autumn Thursday, opened up the boots of various cars and extracted a miscellany of black cases. We proceeded to study instructions as we set up the large tripod, topped with a bright orange lump of metal and glass. Coincidentally we'd also bought a laser measuring device that we promptly experimented with on everything in sight. If we'd put white overalls on we'd have looked like we were setting up a forensic investigation centre!

THEODOLITES IN ARCHAEOLOGICAL SURVEYING

An ancient, long gone settlement often survives in the form of humps and bumps in the landscape and several such areas have been identified around Thriplow, notably in the meadow adjacent to the school, and the field further along towards Fowlmere. In order to form a basis for trying to identify the nature of the settlement, and, possibly, for further geophysical exploration, it is necessary to create a plan of these features.

This is done by means of a plane table, as described in Trail 1. However, in order to obtain precise data on the relative heights and positions of these features it is necessary to use a **theodolite.** This is essentially a low power telescope mounted on a base, which can swivel both in the horizontal and vertical planes. This is mounted on a tripod and has to be precisely levelled (using the built-in spirit level) before it can be used to make accurate height measurements.

Ideally, these should be carried out using a known, fixed height as the "benchmark". These are denoted on OS maps, as a height, and on the ground by the arrow symbol. In practice it is rarely possible to have such a benchmark conveniently located so it is necessary to create a datum point fixed on some immovable object. It is very important that these stationary points are indeed stationary. An early mistake made by the Thriplow group was to fix a datum point against a water trough, only to return some time later to find that this had been moved! The height, in the precise horizontal plane, is first measured from a calibrated surveyors staff held at the chosen stationary datum point, the telescopic sight being focused in the exact horizontal plane, onto the scale. This has now fixed a relative height, against which heights from nearby locations can be directly compared.

Having obtained this fixed height measurement, the staff can be relocated to another nearby feature (or a position within a feature such as a ditch or a large mound) and a new height measurement made.

The difference between this height measurement from the datum point is then noted. Thus a series of height differences in the area being surveyed can be built up so that the layout of the surveyed area can be mapped onto the plane table chart. It is also necessary to measure the distances from each feature to the theodolite, which can either be done with a measuring tape, or with a modern electronic device utilising a low powered laser.

The use of a theodolite is not difficult but it does require considerable care in correctly setting up, but this will become easier with practice!

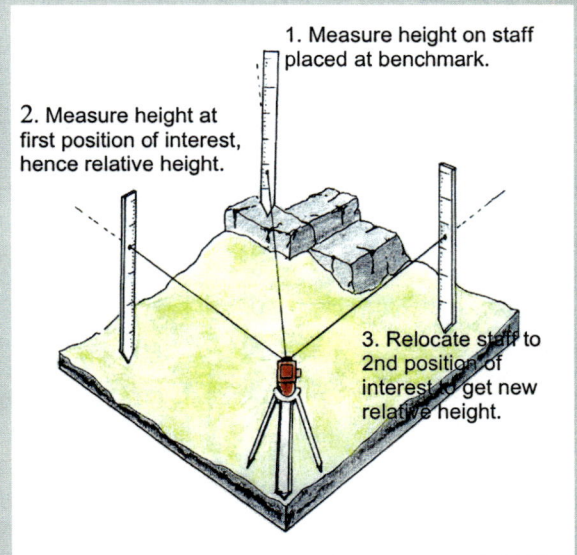

1. Measure height on staff placed at benchmark.

2. Measure height at first position of interest, hence relative height.

3. Relocate staff to 2nd position of interest to get new relative height.

Having sorted our equipment we were ready to attend to Savages Close, the old name for the site of the village school. In conjunction with the headteacher, we decided that it would be worthwhile sharing our experience with the primary school children of Thriplow. Looking nothing like "Savages" they escaped from their classroom one sunny afternoon to join us for a practical comparison of Roman and modern surveying techniques.

After spending time in class studying the theory of Roman road systems they then learned how to survey the line of a new road across a "hill", from towns which they named *Thripium Magnum* and *Thriplis*. We didn't want to interfere with football played on this grass area the next day, so the children trickled sand from bags to leave a visible line of their road. They also turned shoe boxes into mile posts marked out with Roman numerals, and then enjoyed marching along their new road as soldiers would have done.

Tony Jedrej, Countryside Agency

HOW TO USE A GROMA

The **groma** was an instrument used by the Romans for surveying. Essentially it is an upright stick with pieces of wood fixed on top at right angles to form a cross. Weighted strings hang from the end of each arm of the cross. It enables the straight lines of roads to be plotted even when there are hills in the way.

The **groma** (positioned on top of our imaginary hill) was turned until we could sight along two of the strings towards the starting point **A**.

Then we walked around the **groma** and sighted the other way towards the end point **B**. We moved the position of the **groma** until the strings lined up with **B**. By gradually adjusting the position of the **groma** we were able to get the starting point and the end point in a straight line which the children marked out with a sand trail.

Then, again using the **groma,** we marked out the position and street plan of Roman town at right angles to the road.

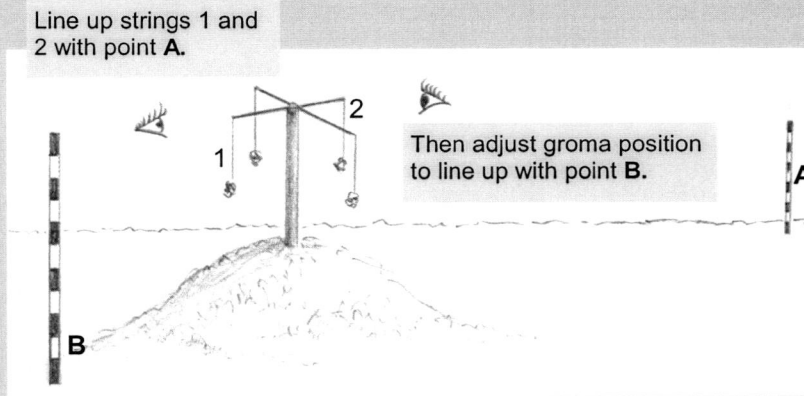

Line up strings 1 and 2 with point **A**.

2

1

Then adjust groma position to line up with point **B**.

A

B

Once they had built their aptly named road *"Via Thriplorum"* they then set about establishing a new settlement at the foot of the "hill", complete with streets set out at right angles and a central forum. This new town was given the name of *Low Campus.*

Whilst these "Roman activities" occupied most of their time the pupils also had a chance to look through the sights of the theodolite and the laser distance measurer. This practical comparison of ancient and modern technology brought 2000 years of surveying activity more closely together and helped them to realise that many of the problems of road building have remained unchanged.

This comparison demonstrated how these ancient techniques were surprisingly accurate. Measurements taken with the groma were almost the same as those using the theodolite.

TRAIL 3
THE QUAVE

The original school building dates back to 1865. Notice the different building styles as it has been extended. The latest additions closely mirror the style and materials shown here.

Walk around the corner looking down over the present school playground.

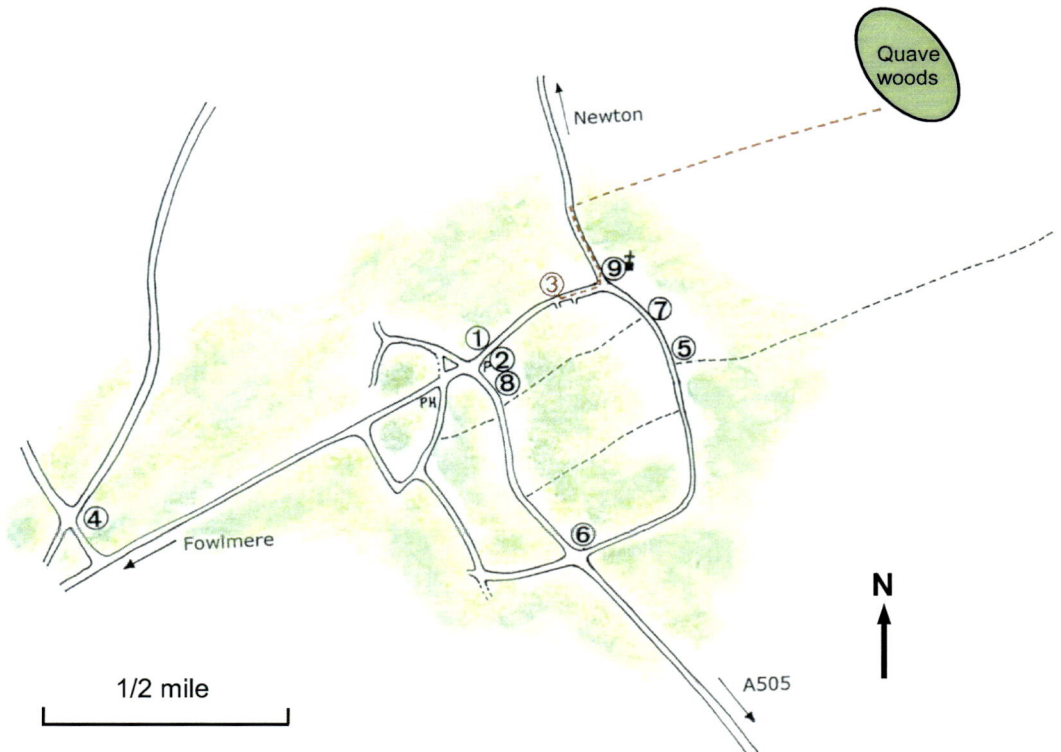

Quave woods

Newton

③

⑨

①
②
⑧

⑦

⑤

PH

④

Fowlmere

⑥

N

A505

1/2 mile

Clunch was used for the floors of houses and for the walls of lower status buildings. It does not resist rain well, eroding easily unless given a protective coating.

Look over the hedge by the bus stop and see the lumpy shape of the disused clunch pit.

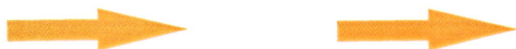

Continue walking along the road towards Newton, then turn right opposite Thriplow Farms buildings.

Follow the permissive path towards the distant woods.

This drawing of the church was made by Nathan Maynard before the restoration of the building in 1855-7. It shows the N.E. end of the church with a lowered North transept and no cockerel on the spire.

Stand by the Quave and look towards the village where you will see the church standing up clearly on the skyline.

Whilst our merry band spends a lot of time prowling the roads and paths of the village, or surveying and logging its features in our search to uncover the village origins, we are very aware that the surrounding landscape is just as important as the village itself.

So it was that we gathered on a fine summer's evening outside the school, ready for a tramp through the countryside. We set off in a crocodile formation up the rise towards the church like a very mature school outing. This wasn't by chance, it was before the bone shaking bumps were installed at the village boundary, and sometimes cars hurtled round the blind corner at the top of the rise!

We couldn't resist a pause by the bus shelter to look down on the field behind the school, to try a different perspective on the ditches we had surveyed there and to reflect on the influence of different ages on the present landscape. A possible medieval moat, a Victorian school and right at our feet a clunch pit. We had already looked at this pit to try and make a guess as to its age, but the only evidence we found was a slightly rotted school jersey, which we suspected might be a later addition rather than a discard from a worker.

After our brief introspection on the field we pressed on down the road towards Newton. The high hedges up to the Newton to Fowlmere toll road make this

Thriplow lies on low Chalk hills which run in a SW/NE direction. Lower Chalk (shown mid-green in the figures opposite) forms the lower land to the north, while the slightly harder Middle Chalk (pale green) forms the higher land in the south of the parish.

There are hard and fissured layers within the Chalk. The Totternhoe Stone, also known as Burwell Rock (shown in dark green in the section diagram), occurs within the Lower Chalk at about 23 metres below the ground surface. The springs in the centre of Thriplow mostly rise from the Totternhoe Stone, since the Chalk Marl below is impermeable. The band of Melbourn Rock with belemnite marls at its base (also shown in dark green) is two or three metres thick. It lies at the boundary of the Lower and Middle Chalk and forms the local highpoint of the village at the church.

The gravel deposits are shown in orange/brown, yellow and pink. The gravel was originally brought from the north by glaciers and various processes and has subsequently been re-distributed (see Gravel Deposits in Trail 6).

More details are in the appendix.

stretch slightly frustrating when you want to consider the landscape in context, but because we had spent some time studying aerial photographs, we paused frequently by any gaps on our left looking for signs of the pingos we knew were there. Equally well there were many pauses on the right where we knew there were lots of field marks showing activity in the area for thousands of years.

THE GEOLOGY OF THE THRIPLOW AREA

KEY

MIDDLE CHALK

LOWER CHALK

HARD CHALK LAYER

TAELE GRAVELS

RIVER GRAVELS

GLACIAL GRAVELS

ALLUVIUM

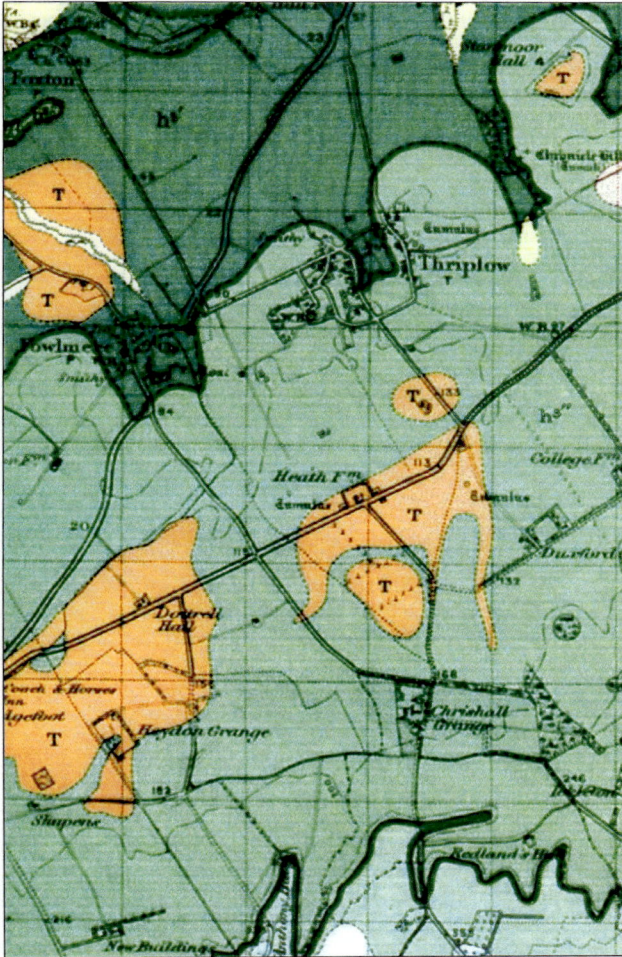

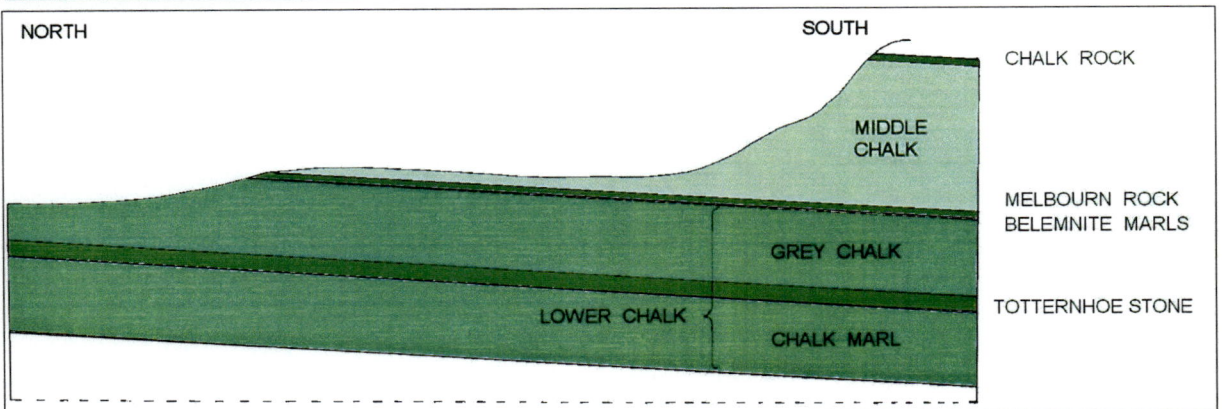

NORTH   SOUTH

CHALK ROCK

MIDDLE CHALK

MELBOURN ROCK
BELEMNITE MARLS

GREY CHALK

TOTTERNHOE STONE

LOWER CHALK

CHALK MARL

Diagram of North/South section through chalk layers. Not to scale and vertical scale exaggerated for clarity.

We wound our way to the outskirts of Newton. This was our initial target because we knew from the aerial photographs that the field back towards Thriplow was covered in crop marks. There was no crop in the field, so off we set for a bit of unstructured field walking. We were looking for any evidence supporting the vast array of field marks from the photographs.

You wouldn't believe how many bits of stone and flint you pass doing this sort of exercise. Any one could be a worked tool, or flakes from flint knapping, or a loom weight or something interesting. Apart from the interesting "token" the total bag was 3 fragments of Victorian or later pottery, half a dozen interesting flints, and several aching backs. This was generally regarded as normal, our group works on hope rather than expectation! Still, the next turn of the plough might turn up some Neolithic flints, a stone axe, a Roman dice or some Anglo-Saxon coins.

Systematic field walking, rather like a forensic team looking for evidence, would be a better way of studying a particular site, but our motivation at the time was simple curiosity.

The tracks between the fields in this area were well marked and in good condition, so having sated our desire to scrutinise the ground we pressed on towards the Quave.

TOKENS

Tokens of the type found in the field to the north of the church were in quite widespread use in the 15th and 16th centuries throughout much of England. We were very fortunate in being able to get the opinion of an authoritative local expert Professor Peter Spufford of Cambridge University.

He told us that they were used by merchants and government officials as counters before "arabic" numerals came into common use in the late 16th century. They were sold in packs made in the Liege area and in Nuremberg around 1600. Curiously, the other reported usage of these tokens was as a coinage, having a value of around one penny.

This seems to tie in with the German nickname of these as "Apfelpfennige" or apple pennies, in reference to the orb on the inscription side. It seems probable that the local squire bought a job lot of these and used them as payment to his servants/employees to spend at the local shops/pubs owned by you know who.

Peter Spufford's fascinating description of the Thriplow token and its origins is in the appendix.

Contrary to what might be expected from a look at the Ordnance Survey map, this long but narrow wooded area is almost impenetrable, being very boggy and jungly.

The wood borders the area known as the Quave, so called because the ground quivers when jumped on. The underlying peat makes the ground feel springy. A dictionary definition shows "*quaven*" to be a word of Germanic origin meaning "to tremble".

Peat Holes in Thriplow

This map came from G.O.Vinter's papers, c.1950, in the Cambridge Record Office, reference 299. North is at the top of the map.

The caption at the bottom reads

O= willows planted by G.O.Vs father
Shaded area =general area where Peat Holes were formerly.

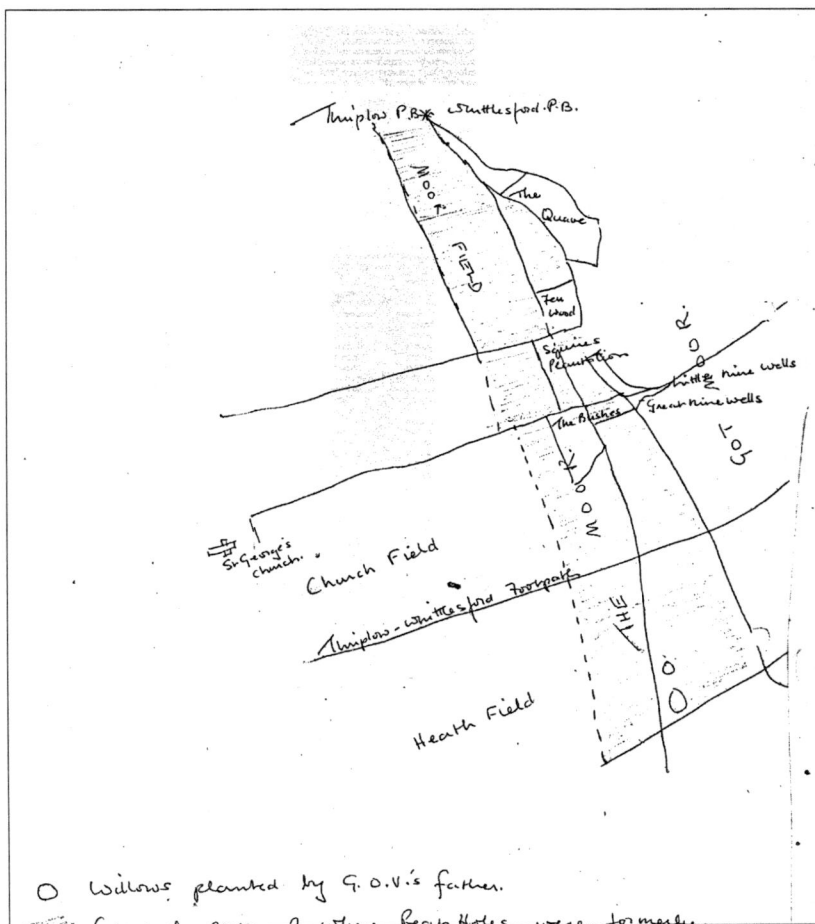

TRAIL 4
THE SHRIMP POND

You may be lucky enough to find one of the rare fairy shrimps for which this area of Cambridgeshire is noted. They are 1-2 cm. long, diaphanous green in colour and swim upside down. As the shrimps are transparent, food can be seen in their gut.

Stand at the crossroads and look into the corner of the field. After a period of wet weather you might see a temporary pond.

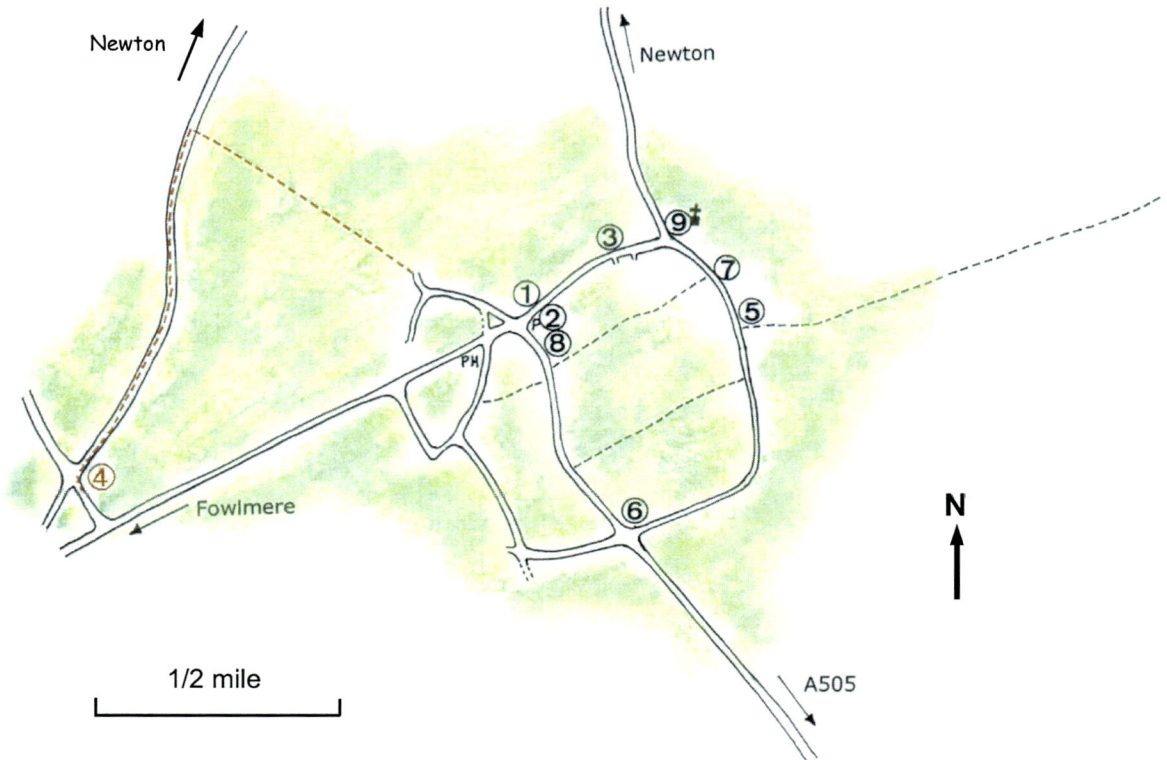

Newton

Newton

Fowlmere

1/2 mile

N

A505

These oyster shells may have been the remains of a meal nearly 2000 years ago.

Look in the field to the N.W. of this road to see where there was once an Iron Age/Roman settlement.

Walk along the wide verge of the old turnpike road towards Newton.

As you walk along the road to Newton look for a slight rise in the ground on your left. Is this a continuation of the Bran Ditch, a defensive earthwork running from the wooded heights of Heydon to the marshy ground at Fowlmere?

Near the redundant telephone exchange a path leading South-East from this road will take you back to Thriplow. It lies opposite the line of the old track to Foxton which is marked on R.G.Baker's 1821 map.

VIII
MILES TO
CAMBRIDGE

A. D.
MDCCXXX

Notice the milestone on the North side of the road.

In 1586 Dr William Mowse, the then Master, left money to Trinity Hall, Cambridge for a series of milestones to be built. They were set up in the early 18th century, decorated with the arms of Mowse and the college. Measuring from Great St.Mary's church in Cambridge to London they are the earliest milestones in England, apart from Roman examples.

Page 41

The meeting point of the parish boundaries of Foxton, Fowlmere and Thriplow is a little microcosm of history. There is large hollow in a field, the remains of an Ice Age pingo, extensive Iron Age crop marks, peculiar indentations in the parish boundary, possibly Saxon, wide 18th century road verges, and even the parish boundary with Foxton has changed within the last 50 years. All in all it looks like a fairly innocuous rural crossroads, but with this wealth of historical fabric we just had to visit.

First we walked to a network of lanes towards Fowlmere to see if there were any features that would explain the square shape jutting out of the Fowlmere parish boundary. Not so straightforward because some houses had been built since the latest edition of the 1:25000 map we were using. Apparently our group was noticed by one of the householders no doubt wondering what this strange group was about. He was soon soothed, as most people are interested in their local history as long as it doesn't presage a supermarket being built nearby.

There was no obvious geographical reason for the anomalous boundary so whilst ambling back we speculated over the land ownership of the Round Moat site nearby in Fowlmere having an influence.

When we approached our cars we couldn't fail to see a police car parked nearby. Seeing a police car at all in the rural environs is rare, parked next to us, it was a cause for concern. Looking back you've got to admire the courage of the policeman standing his ground as our group approached, because, as it turns out, he thought we were a group of hare coursers setting up for an event!

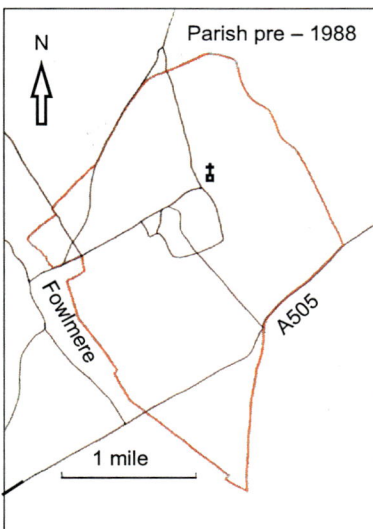

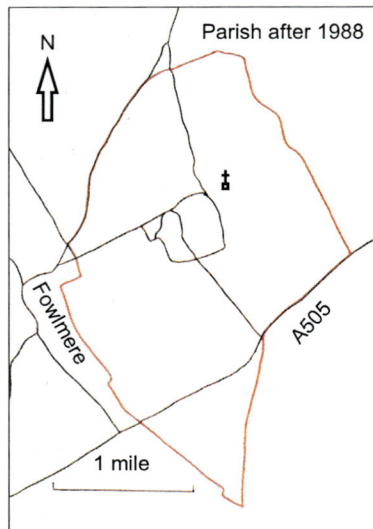

Thriplow parish boundaries.

These two maps show the boundary changes in the West of the parish where it borders the parish of Fowlmere. In 1988 Little Thriplow became part of Fowlmere parish.

The wealth of interest in this area led to another longer visit, this time with a natural history theme. Abutting the cross-roads, in the field to the east of the small telephone exchange, there is a marked depression which sometimes becomes a pond after a wet spell. This is the remains of a pingo, which in this case as one of the 'transient pools of Cambridgeshire' has evolved its own ecology.

THE DEVELOPMENT OF A PINGO

Pingo scars are a remnant of a time when Thriplow was in the grip of severe periglacial conditions during the Ice Ages. Pingos are conical shaped hills with an inner core of ice. Pingos (an Inuit word) occur in areas of intense cold, such as the Arctic region, where the ground is frozen with many metres of permafrost.

The pingos at Thriplow were formed as a result of spring activity. The pressure of the groundwater in the Chalk hills to the south of Thriplow forces springs to rise from the hard and fissured Totternhoe Stone. The spring water freezes into a lens of ice as it nears the surface, and this will gradually grow as the spring feeds it, pushing the ground above it into a conical shaped hill.

Even in such cold conditions, the sun's radiation causes the temperature of the ground surface to fluctuate on a daily and annual basis, causing some surface melting. The frozen ground contains a large proportion of ice and on melting the mixture of soil and meltwater will flow down slope. Consequently, the soil covering the ice core of the pingo will gradually slip down the sides, forming a ring of debris around it. Eventually during a thaw the ice core will melt leaving a circular depression in the ground surrounded by a raised ring, known as a pingo scar, a fossil pingo or even an 'ognip'! Where the spring persists, a pond will form in the fossil pingo depression.

It is likely that the pingos scars we now see in Thriplow were created more than 10,000 years ago – geologically speaking, very recently!

More details are in the appendix.

1. After Ice Lens Formed

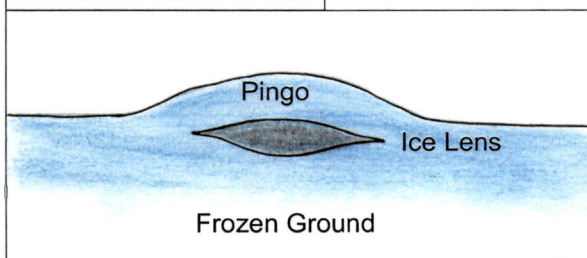

Pingo
Ice Lens
Frozen Ground

2. Summer Thaws

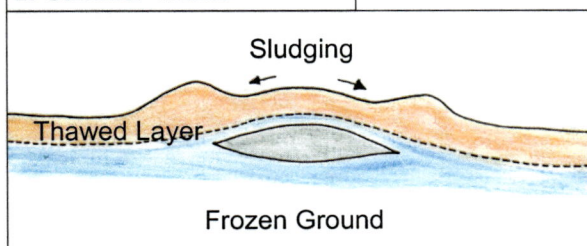

Sludging
Thawed Layer
Frozen Ground

3. On Finally Melting

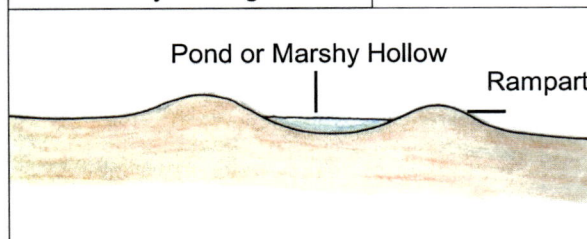

Pond or Marshy Hollow
Rampart

The pingo is the home of the "Red Book" endangered species *Chirocephalus diaphanous* or fairy shrimp which survives periods of drought by encysting itself in the mud, a bit like dried yeast, then emerges when the pool is filled.

This robust environment is also the home to a rare plant, the hyssop leaved loosestrife *Lythrum hyssopifolia*.

The whole area abounds with these depressions and on aerial photographs the cropmarks show very early man made tracks that wound around these features to avoid their boggy nature.

Hyssop leaved loosestrife.

Walton Common, east of King's Lynn, is a low lying area of rough grazing on the margin between permeable chalk and impermeable clay. The features of depressions and ramparts formed at the end of the last glacial period here remain undisturbed by ploughing. Maybe this is what parts of Thriplow would have looked like too.

We have a wide ranging and enthusiastic approach to things in the landscape, but none of us have the abilities of David Bellamy so we approached our pond equipped simply with wellies, fishing nets, jam jars and a magnifying glass intent on seeing one of these small creatures.

A shallow pond seemed like a straightforward paddle out, get a sample, have a look, and put it back sort of task. We'd failed to appreciate fully that although a pingo remnant tends to fill with peat, the surrounding soil was clay. Our first wader lost his boot within a few

yards and from then on we took samples from the edge!

We didn't find the shrimp but consoled ourselves with the thought that something almost 2 cm long and nearly transparent, moving around in muddy water, might be tricky to see anyway!

Moving forward in time from the Ice Ages we physically moved on to the field opposite on the north side of the Fowlmere - Newton road. The aerial photographs of this field show crop marks that look like the edges of tracks by-passing pingos and other linear marks. These could be anything from Stone Age to medieval constructions but are thought to be Iron Age. From a field walking perspective this is not promising but worth a look for bits of pottery, or earlier evidence of worked flints. We found nothing of interest apart from an oyster shell - probably the cast off from a Roman (or Victorian) roadside snack!

As we progressed northwards across the recently harvested field, we reached the line of the old Foxton -Thriplow parish boundary. This is a substantial bank between the fields on either side on a small natural rise in the ground, also noticeable as you go up the road to Foxton. Rowland Parker cited this as an extension of the Heydon (Bran) ditch, one of the ditches dug across Cambridgeshire in the Saxon period, (6th century or so).

The bank is there and might indeed have been a barrier between the Fowl mere and Dry mere, the area to the north east around Hoffers brook. Until someone excavates and finds some datable artefacts, it is as good a reason as any for the existence of the bank.

We slowly progressed back to the Fowlmere - Newton road and rested on the wide grassy banks. In fact the roadside verges on both sides are wider than the road itself. This brought us historically much nearer to our own time, when this was the main Cambridge to London toll road. An entrepreneurial activity then was to waylay coaches, reap their wealth and make off into the distance. One of the ways of limiting this was to remove the shelter by the edge of the road by making broad open verges, allowing the coach driver time to respond to the highwayman's threat. There's still no place to hide by this road!

Travelling up the road towards Newton we came across a milestone, placed here in about 1730 at the bequest of Dr William Mowse of Trinity Hall, to comfort the weary traveller by telling him there were only 8 miles left to go to Cambridge, and presumably sanctuary. Our destination on this occasion was the Green Man in Thriplow, and about 600m further on towards Newton we took the permissive footpath on the right leading across the fields directly to our own 'sanctuary'.

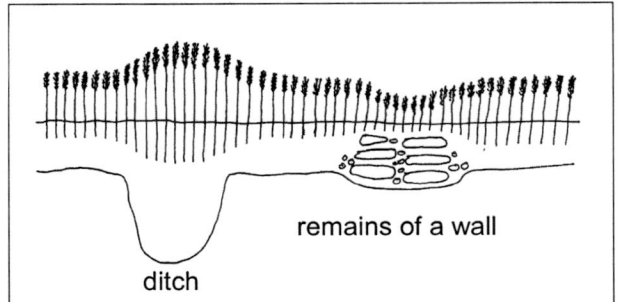

remains of a wall

ditch

AERIAL PHOTOGRAPHY

Aerial photography reveals crop marks caused by a variety of processes e.g. variations in geology, agricultural practices, archaeological features. During dry periods buried remains have an effect on the crops growing above them, in particular on cereal crops.

The diagram shows in simplified form the effects of an old ditch and wall underlying a crop of wheat.

Where there has been a ditch, even when levelled by ploughing, the soil is richer and more moist and the crop will ripen more quickly....as in the diagram above. Conversely, where there is underlying stone work the soil will be thinner and drier which will delay ripening. Drought years show these effects even more.

Oblique aerial photograph of the area directly North of the trail starting point.

Source....University of Cambridge Aerial Photography Collection.

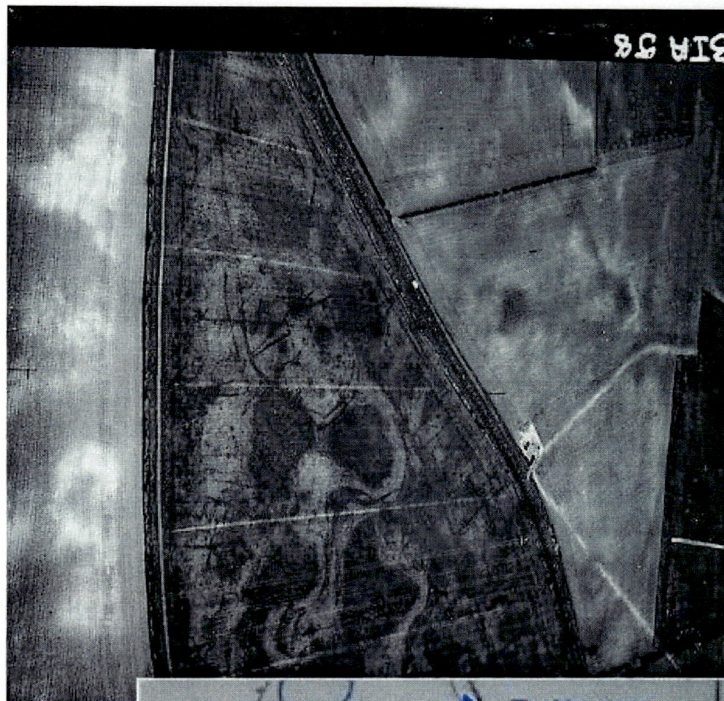

Man made features identified in the photograph above.

Showing clearly are pits, and circular and double edged track like features. Some of these respect the differential drainage of the pingos, following around the raised edges and avoiding the damper hollows which appear darker in the photograph.

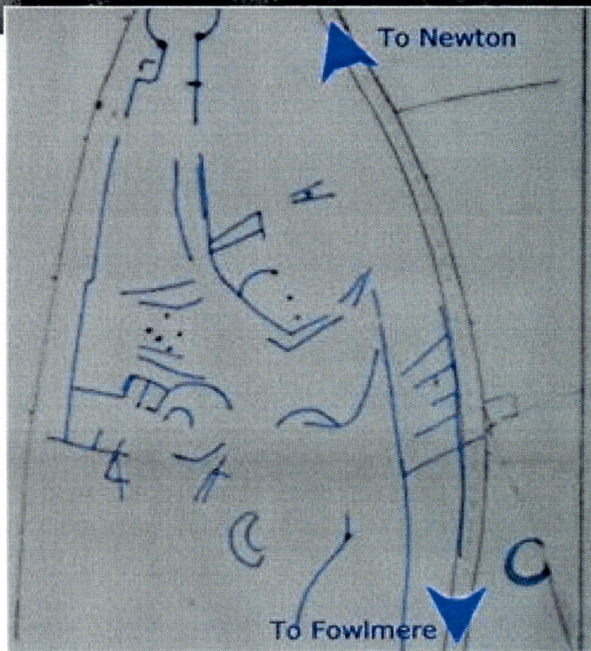

To Newton

To Fowlmere

TRAIL 5
DRIFT TRACK

This track follows the general direction of an ancient routeway, Ashwell Street, which goes SW-NE towards Norfolk.

Walk under the large walnut tree, once important not only as a food source but for foraging animals. Along this trail count the number of species found in the hedge on the right of the path.

Wild Rose has a delicate pale pink flower.

Blackthorn or sloe has narrow dark green leaves.

To the left of the path look for a slight dip in the field. Is this evidence of the old Mutlow Way, a *hollow way*, which ran towards Newton?

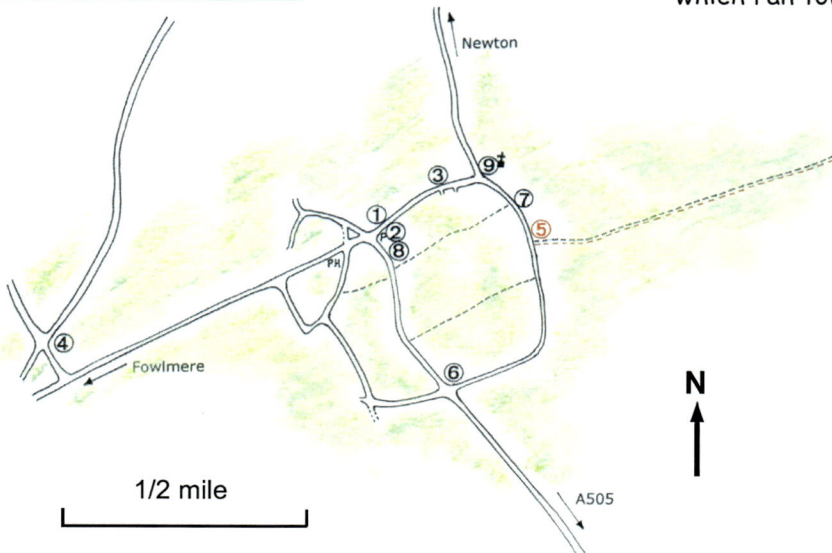

Newton

③ ⑨
① ⑦
②
⑧ ⑤
PH

④
Fowlmere ⑥

N

1/2 mile

A505

Look towards the high ground near the church. A slight rise in the ground indicates the site of a Bronze Age tumulus.

The brick structure on the right of the path is a pill box, a war time relic.

Cross a small ditch and notice the rising ground where on the left is the site of a Roman villa. Nearby in the woods are the natural springs at Nine Wells.
A permissive footpath leads North from here and can be followed into the edge of the village of Whittlesford.

Shortly before turning back the buildings and aircraft of Duxford Museum are clearly visible. Contrast the ancient line of Ashwell Street you are standing on with the vista of the M11 below.

The Drift is a well used path running between Thriplow and Whittlesford. Nowadays the main traffic is farm vehicles and cars full of anglers heading for the fishing lake part of the way along. Our group has regularly wandered up and down this old pathway with its curious juxtaposition of the ancient and the modern.

The modern is easy to sort out, 200 yards down the path is a WW2 brick pill box guarding the outer margins of the Duxford airfield easily visible to the south.

The ancient is much more difficult to discern. The path itself, follows the direction of Icknield Way or Ashwell Street, a major trade route no doubt for flints from Grimes Graves in Norfolk and all sorts of goods to and from the coast to the Cotswolds. It's easy to imagine how more than 250 generations of traders could have followed the same route, with very little change up to 100 years ago.

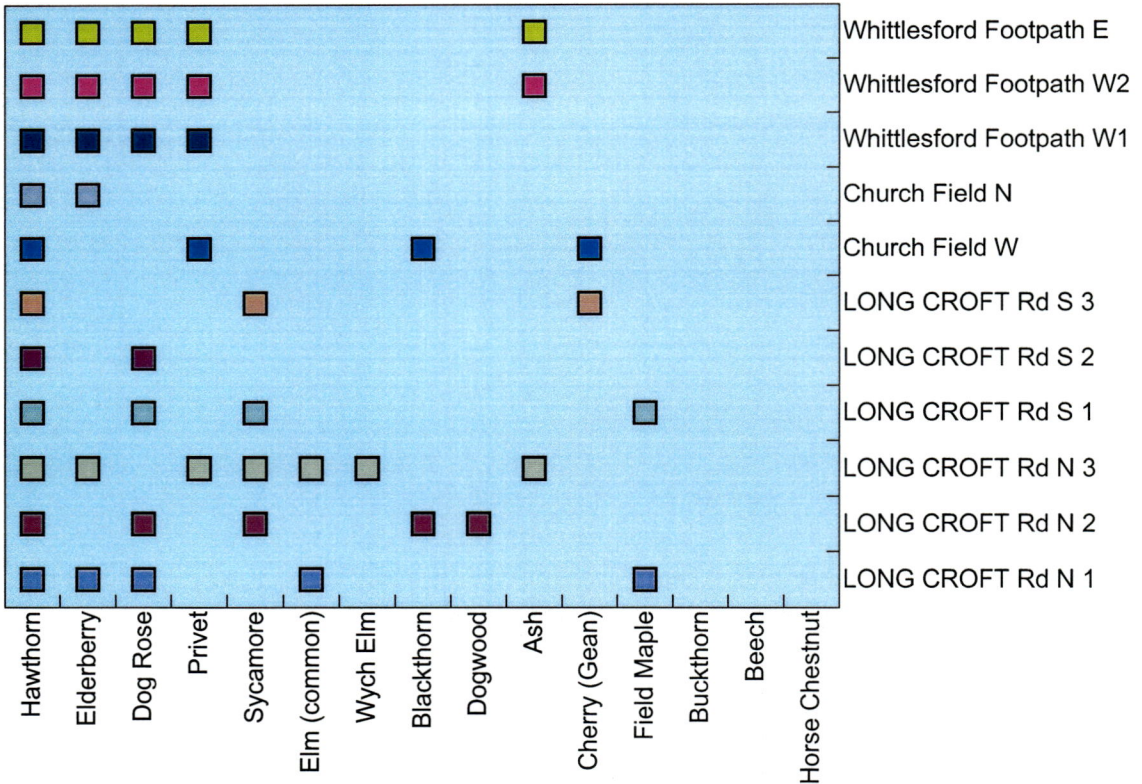

	Hawthorn	Elderberry	Dog Rose	Privet	Sycamore	Elm (common)	Wych Elm	Blackthorn	Dogwood	Ash	Cherry (Gean)	Field Maple	Buckthorn	Beech	Horse Chestnut
Whittlesford Footpath E	X	X	X	X						X					
Whittlesford Footpath W2	X	X	X	X						X					
Whittlesford Footpath W1	X	X	X	X											
Church Field N	X	X													
Church Field W	X				X			X			X				
LONG CROFT Rd S 3	X				X						X				
LONG CROFT Rd S 2	X		X												
LONG CROFT Rd S 1	X		X		X							X			
LONG CROFT Rd N 3	X	X			X	X	X	X			X				
LONG CROFT Rd N 2	X		X		X			X	X						
LONG CROFT Rd N 1	X	X	X					X				X			

Plant species in samples of hedgerows in Thriplow.

HEDGE DATING

Hedges are one of the prime elements which help to define and enliven the rural landscape. Hedges have been used for many centuries as one of the means of marking boundaries, for dividing up land use or for preventing livestock from straying. In medieval England, hedges were very important and prominent features.

Several different methods were used to make hedges. If the plants used were alive and transplanted from elsewhere, then it was a 'living hedge'. Conversely, there were also 'dead hedges', comprising simply interwoven stakes or poles and they might well have included cut thorns as well. Frequently, quickthorns (hawthorn) were used alone, especially by the surveyors and promoters of the Acts of Enclosure, carried through over many years up until the late 19th century. Occasionally other plant species were interspersed in hedges or became established naturally within the original hedge line.

Following much study and research on hedges, a method known as Hooper's Rule, was devised during the 1970's, to enable hedges to be dated. It is named after its inventor, Dr. Max Hooper.

Hooper's Rule proposes that within a 30 yard length of hedge, the number of tree or shrub species found is equal to the age of the hedge in centuries. A very simple example illustrates this: if four species are found in a 30 yard length of hedge, then the hedge is most likely about 400 years old. The term 'most likely' has been included here, as Hooper's Rule works better in certain areas rather than others. It is useful in planned countryside, such as Lincolnshire, Huntingdonshire and parts of other counties including Cambridgeshire.

An attempt was made recently to date some of the hedges in Thriplow, using Hooper's Rule. Some hedges, such as those along Long Croft, which formed the edge of an old plantation, gave very high counts of plant species, indicating great age. However, Church Field and the Whittlesford footpath gave lower counts of species, indicating younger hedges.

The most frequently found hedge plant was Hawthorn, followed by Elderberry, Dog-Rose, Privet and Sycamore. Amongst the least frequent were Dogwood, Wych Elm, Buckthorn, and Beech.

Thus, following Hooper's Rule, Lower Street, with up to 11 species per 30 yards, possesses the oldest hedges, possibly up to 1000 years old, whilst Church Field, with between 2 to 5 species per 30 yards contains the youngest hedges, possibly a mere 200 to 400 years old.

So much for theory - how do you set about proving it? We're used to standing out in the landscape and this outing was no different. After measuring several 30 yard lengths along the track, we spread ourselves out and plunged into the hedgeline. Not so odd, just different!

The aim was to count the number of species within these lengths to estimate the age of the hedge. Despite some of our members being less botanically adept than others all in all the data suggested that the hedge was about 500 years old.

Moving a little way off the track, after some discussions with the paddock owners, we found ourselves on several occasions investigating the site of a tumulus. This was real antiquity, dated to about 1500B.C. by an excavation done in 1953, and now scarcely visible on the ground. The mound has been almost completely obliterated by successive ploughing. Aerial photographs still show a crop mark and our resistivity testing clearly showed where the ditch was placed. More details are in the appendix.

Artist's impression of the tumulus.

THE NAMING OF THRIPLOW

Why is Thriplow called Thriplow?
Now that is an interesting question. Most people take for granted the name of the town or village where they live but there is often a history associated with place names. In our case can we work out any meaning in the word 'Thriplow'?
A study of philology, which is the investigation of the structure and history of words, can show us some clues as to how the name became established. But first of all we need to put a time-scale in place. We know absolutely nothing about what people living in the area during the Stone Age right through to the Anglo-Saxons called where they lived. So it is not until around 600 to 700 AD that we start to get an inkling of names being associated with places. Even during Roman times we do not know what vast tracks of the country were called, only some towns are written into the records.
As it happens the Anglo-Saxons had a very good eye for features in the landscape and so they allocated words to places that described where they had settled.

So it seems that the part of a place name with the syllable 'low' in it signifies a burial mound, and in our case it is thought to refer to the mound of tumulus found in the field by the present day church in Thriplow as it still, most likely, retained its prominence in the landscape.
The other part of the word seems to be associated with a proper name; perhaps a person called *Trippa* who is assumed to be interred in the tumulus. There is certainly no evidence for this so this part of the name is likely to remain a mystery.
During the time of the Normans the name in the Domesday Book is recorded as *Trepeslau* and survived the vagaries of mediaeval spellings to enter the 19th century as *Triplow*. It wasn't until the beginning of the last century that it became standardised as Thriplow – quite a journey!

We don't know if goats were around when this particular burial mound was dug, but they certainly were when we were trying to take our measurements. Although she was fairly friendly, we rapidly discovered that a goat's view of our presence was to provide entertaining new toys, such as tapes or cables to chew on, or people to play chase with!

We also checked out the site with our metal detector. This piece of equipment is, archaeologically speaking, a mixed blessing. In disturbed soil where there is no 'context' it is very useful for finding metal coins or buckles or other items easily missed. 'Context' means an identifiable section of soil where other material may be present.

For example if you find a dateable coin in a layer of darker soil when soil above and below is lighter, you can be reasonably sure that anything else in that dark layer is of a similar age to the coin. If someone comes along and just digs out the coin you lose the context, or if it's a brooch you can't relate it to the pottery that may be in the same layer.

There's also the problem of treasure. There have been cases of people searching for coins or other metal artefacts just for financial gain, not dissimilar to the Egyptian tomb robbers. Hopefully the introduction of the Portable Antiquities Scheme and the Treasure Act will reduce the impact of this, or at the very least allow finds to be recorded so that not all the information is lost.

In our investigation of the tumulus we found several Roman coins in the topsoil of the private paddocks - all noted now in the Sites and Monuments Records - but none in the relatively open field area. Their dates span over 400 years of Roman occupation.

THE LAW AND THE ARCHAEOLOGIST

After a series of damning press articles in which metal detectorists were deemed to be responsible for wrecking archaeological sites, the Government decided to bring in 'The Treasure Act' of 1996 that became law on 24th September 1997. It replaced the common law position on treasure trove.

The Act offers definitions of treasure and gives finders instructions on what to do about their finds. It also has teeth in that failure to report could mean a fine of up to £5,000 and or a three-month spell in clink!

To help in organising the new system local councils are urged to employ 'Finds Liaison Officers' whose job is to receive artefacts, not only treasure, and ensure that proper records are kept of when and where the objects were found.

So next time you dig up a hoard of gold coins in your back garden, ignorance of the law is no excuse if you are tempted to pocket the lot!

Details of reported finds are published on the web at www.finds.org.uk.

Agrippa dupondius 63-12 B.C.

Reverse ….Neptune standing with a trident S.C.

25mm. diameter 8.467g

Vespasian dupondius A.D. 69-79

Obverse…….radiate head, inscription IMP. CAES.VESPASIAN.AVG.COS.III

Reverse…….probably shows Fortuna or Felicitas standing. S.C.

27mm. diameter   9.658g

Trajan as A.D. 98-117

Obverse……..inscription IMP.TRIANO AVG. GER.DAC.P.M.TR.COS.VI.P.P.

Reverse……. probably shows Fortuna standing. S.C.

25mm. diameter   12.117g

Constans   A.D. 337-390

Obverse…….draped bust inscription CONSTANS AVG

Reverse…….two soldiers standing either side of standard, inscription GLORIA EXERCITVS

14mm. diameter approximately   0.971g

Coins kindly identified by Chris Montague from the Archaeological Field Unit

On the parish border between Thriplow and Whittlesford the Ordnance Survey map shows 'Little Nine Wells' and 'Great Nine Wells'. Older editions show 'Chronicle Hills' and 'tumuli' in the same place, and an aerial photograph we were shown indicated very clearly that this was the site of a Roman Villa.

The site itself is a Scheduled Monument, even though there is nothing visible in the field itself. This means that there are all sorts of restrictions on disturbing the site apart from normal farming, and even that can be affected for example by controlling the depth of ploughing. Luckily we are not an invasive bunch so we decided to try out some resistivity measurement on the areas which were unclear in the photograph. It didn't look very far from the field access road to the site, and the landowners had let us take a car as near as possible but we were all ready for a rest by the time we had carted all our gear to the site.

Once we got going though, the work progressed briskly for a time then slowed down dramatically as we passed from a bare mud surface to where the young sugarbeet crop was growing. We had no problems taking our readings between the reasonably spaced plants and the farmer, watching from the side, wasn't concerned over our activities, the problem was the wire.

To work the equipment it needs a 50m cable to some remote point, and holding this above the plants proved both difficult and tiring! Every individual plant seemed, after a while, to be intent on holding on to the cable! We persisted and got the readings eventually but the trek back seemed much further than the way there!

Photograph with kind permission from Syngenta

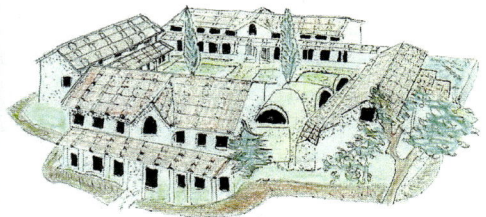

Drawing of what the villa may have looked like. Renate Milner.

THE ROMAN VILLA PLAN

In the Roman world, the term 'villa' generally referred to a farm and its outbuildings. However, today the term means a house built in the country in the Roman style. The resident may have been a local Romanised landowner or farmer, or a Roman official seeking a country residence away from the hustle and bustle of town or city. Many villas seemed to be sited away from other habitations and were positioned, wherever possible, so as to provide pleasant views and, essentially, a ready water supply nearby. Often they had gardens, in which flowers and herbs were cultivated, and sometimes there were decorative water features as well. Many of the Roman villas so far discovered in this country are sited in the lowland areas of Britain.

There are several hundred known villa sites in Britain, built over a period of perhaps 400 years. In many cases, over this time, villas underwent modifications to the layout and function, due to changing needs of the owners. Consequently, villa plans developed in many different ways according to the changing status and wealth of the owner or simply due to changing fashions.

Villas were generally well built and many of the higher-status ones possessed elegant decorations. Brightly painted wall plaster added colour to the main rooms, together with tiles or mosaics, and floors were often tessellated. Some of these were quite complex in design, and depicted mythological scenes or perhaps symbolic and floral patterns.

The majority of Roman villas in Britain were single-storied structures and had a series of rooms placed in wings. The most frequently met type is the winged corridor house. Some of the rooms were for living or sleeping, or other domestic functions. However, many villas were provided with a suite of hot and cold baths. The pleasant whiling away of time in these rooms represented a major aspect of Roman social life, and the process of bathing was an elaborate activity, in town or country.

Central heating was provided by a hypocaust system, which involved warm air from an outside furnace being channelled through a series of flues running under floors and in the walls of buildings.

A fairly general and simple Roman villa plan is included here, as an example. This plan is based on a villa in Oxfordshire, and may represent a type of plan common during the second century AD.

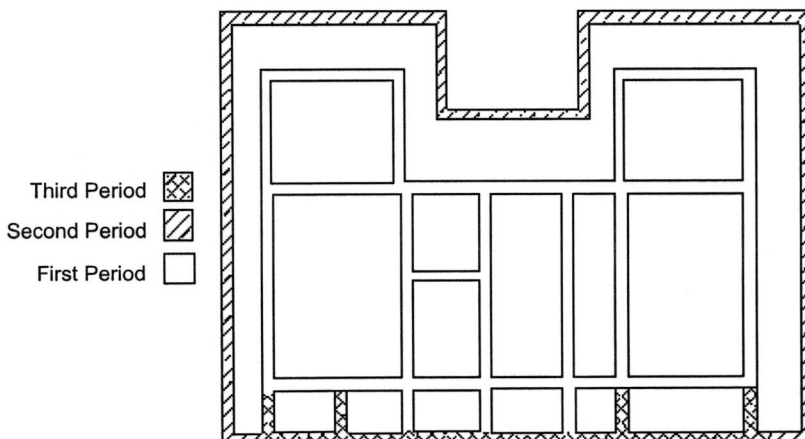

Third Period
Second Period
First Period

Plan of a typical Second century Roman villa.

On the way down the Drift with its Bronze Age tumulus, where the eponymous Trippa may have been buried, its Roman villa and its modern pillbox, you can't help thinking about the in between bit. It survived straightening during the Enclosure but that still leaves about 1000 years without any mark on the landscape. Maybe that's because the cycle of days, seasons and trade didn't change appreciably for the farming community using this route.

The first documentary evidence does point to one other facet of this particular area, if not to do with the track itself. The earliest known administrative groups in Cambridgeshire were called Hundreds. From the tenth century Thriplow Hundred comprised the parishes of Thriplow, Fowlmere, Foxton, Hauxton, Harston, Newton, Great and Little Shelford, Stapleford and Trumpington. Hundred courts met every four weeks when items of common interest or dispute could be sorted out. The Hundred may at one stage have referred to an area of 100 hides (12,000 acres), a hide being 120 acres. Its equivalent in Danelaw was the 'Wapentake' which meant "weapon touch" presumably what happened when a vote was taken.

It is possible that the Thriplow Hundred meeting place was the old tumulus, in which case no doubt the meetings were short with the participants standing on a windswept hill! This would account for the association of 'Mutlow Hill' with the site, 'Mutlow' being a corruption of Moot Law (*moot* meaning meeting).

THRIPLOW HUNDRED

The hundred was a form of local government in England, at which representatives from each constituent parish met to administer justice and settle local problems. It existed, as an institution, from early Saxon times until the 19th century. The term 'hundred' may have originally referred to a hundred hides. A hide was the unit of land supposed to support one peasant family. Each hundred meeting comprised a court that met at a well-known time and location, called locally 'the accustomed place,' and the meetings were generally held in the open air. Originally, all the inhabitants of a hundred were expected to attend the meetings, but in time, attendance became restricted to only the more prominent tenants in each parish.

Map of the parishes in Thriplow Hundred

A hundred was established in Thriplow by 1066, and it may have met on the Heath. However, by about the thirteenth century, it is likely that the 'accustomed place' was moved to the more centrally located Newton, as the name 'Mutlowe,' which normally refers to a hundred meeting place, was recorded there from the thirteenth century. The name, Thriplow Hundred, went out of use in the late 19th century.

A number of parishes formed the hundred of Thriplow and in 1845 these were: Trumpington, Great Shelford, Little Shelford, Hauxton, Harston, Newton, Foxton, Fowlmere and Thriplow.

Those who attended the hundred court, known as 'the suitors,' acted as judges, and they heard and awarded judgements on cases brought before them. It is worth noting that in medieval times the hundred was held collectively responsible for certain crimes committed within its borders, if an offender could not be found or brought before the hundred for judgement.

Thus the hundred was considered a very important means of maintaining law and order at a local level and it was visited by the sheriff, twice annually, when he himself generally acted as judge. The sheriff was the King's officer and representative.

TRAIL 6
THE SOUTH SIDE

Just North of the cross roads look
on the East side of the road. There
is an old clunch pit, now almost
overgrown.

Driving out of the village feel
the modern speed bumps before
passing over the fossilised
remains of field headlands, part
of the old 3 field system.

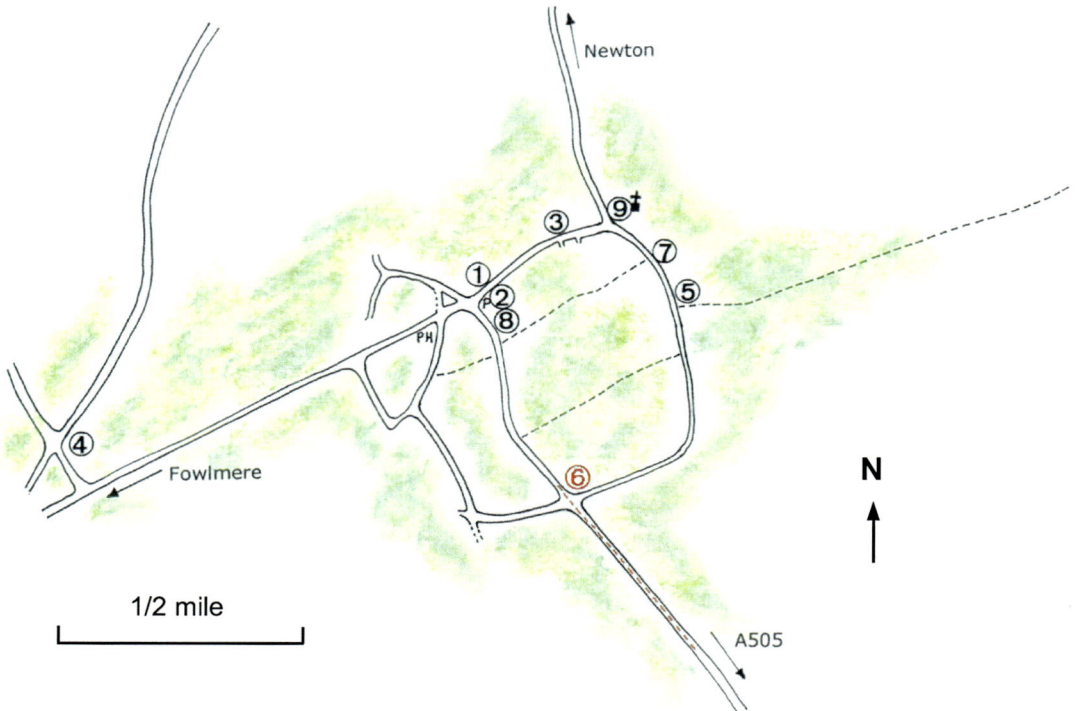

Newton

Fowlmere

1/2 mile

N

A505

At the highest point of the road on your right is the old gravel pit, a valuable resource for the village in the past. Imagine how far just over 30,000 m³ would spread along the road, maybe 18 km!

Turn right on to the A505 after passing the recycling centre.

About 1 mile along the A505 stop in the layby on the right. The Commonwealth army was encamped here in 1641 when it refused to disband during its dispute with Parliament. You are near another of the many tumuli that were arranged along the line of this ancient route.

Follow up some of these leads by visiting.........

Cambridge Museum of Archaeology and Anthropology.

Deserted villages such as Clopton near Croydon, Cambridgeshire.

The County Records Office.

Madingly Hall....... to take an outreach course.

Standing at the crossroads on the outskirts of Thriplow in early springtime, there are two things that leap out at you after a moment's contemplation. If you've timed it right, firstly see the profusion of daffodils in the verges. Planted, tended and nurtured to support the renowned 'Daffodil Weekend' in the village, but the yellow of the daffodils around the village is a modern introduction. In years gone by the village was better known for a saffron colour, being one edge of the golden triangle of the Saffron Crocus. The second thing that stands out is how straight the road to the A505 is, and how undulating.

You would have thought that if they could lay the tarmac in such a straight line, they could have made it smooth as well!

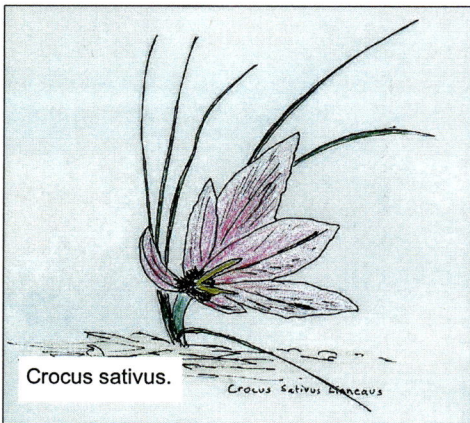
Crocus sativus.

SAFFRON

Saffron (*crocus sativus*) is a pretty flower with six purple petals and three bright orange–red stigma, about 25mm long, protruding from the centre. These stigma are used for their flavouring, colouring, and somewhat controversially, medicinal properties. It has been described as the most precious and expensive spice in the world which may be something of a hyperbole. Nevertheless, its importance as a locally grown crop was considerable

Saffron was used and traded extensively throughout the Middle East in the ancient Grecian era as a spice and as an alleged aphrodisiac. Perhaps it was the price and appearance which conferred the latter property when presented to impressionable young women by optimistic old men! It seems very likely the Romans took it to Britain where it was found to grow well in the Cam valley region with its numerous Roman settlements.

From the 15th until up to the early 19th century local records show it was grown as an important cash crop in the "Golden triangle" which included Thriplow and the eponymous Walden. The harvesting of the saffron was extremely labour intensive as it required the separation of the stigma filaments from the rest of the flower. W. Clarke of Shelford, wrote in 1771 that "the saffron crocus is planted in summer in rows five inches apart, the corms two inches apart about six inches deep " and "an acre of land could employ 10 people for a short season". Around 150,000 flowers were needed to produce 1kg of the filaments, which, on drying, yielded about 200g of the final product, then used as a spice or orange dye.

A combination of effects, including fungal disease, climate change and economic circumstances, led to the cessation of the commercial harvesting of saffron. At the onset of the Industrial Revolution there were more effective ways of earning a living, even though this may have entailed emigrating. It may also be surmised that there was increased competition from the Mediterranean region and China where it was produced more cheaply. Saffron is now only grown commercially in these warmer climates.

Conventional wisdom has it that the Romans built roads in straight lines trampling over everything in sight, (actually they were much more pragmatic and put in kinks where it was sensible), but in this case it is extremely unlikely that the Romans were involved. The saying 'as straight as a ruler' is much nearer the mark because this stretch of road came into being directly as a result of some lowly clerk laying a ruler across a map of the countryside in the early nineteenth century and inscribing a line at the command of the Official Surveyor.

They were possibly in the pay of one of the local landowners intent on - and here you need to sort out your political views - consolidating land use for maximum efficiency of use or consolidating and increasing land holdings for maximum profit: Enclosure.

ENCLOSURE

Thriplow was enclosed by Act of Parliament in 1840. The process took five years and changed the landscape from three wide open fields divided into small strips cultivated by individual landowners in mutual agreement into fields hedged and ditched, each field owned by one person and cultivated by him as he wished. The effect on the landscape was dramatic. Instead of wide open fields, a pattern of smaller hedged fields gave the 'patchwork' effect we think of as traditional. Yet in south Cambridgeshire this pattern is no more than 160 years old.

The process was organised by three Commissioners, a surveyor and a solicitor who acted as secretary to the Commissioners. They measured and divided the land so that each owner received the same acreage as he had before enclosure with the exception of the Vicar and Tithe owner who received extra land in lieu of the tithes they would now lose. Roads were straightened and drained; the Fowlmere Road and the road to the A505 rise and fall revealing the pre-enclosure Headlands under the tarmac. Farming continued but under the direction of the Commissioners until the whole process was complete. The Moor, which had been common, was divided up between the landowners depriving the labourers of fuel and fodder. All they were left with was 2 acres of Recreation Ground.

The open-field landscape which had been cultivated in common since late Saxon or early Norman times was changed to the landscape we recognise today. Land had become private property.

Before 1840 the agricultural pattern of Thriplow was similar to the Champion landscape of Southern England. Virtually all the land around the village was divided into three huge fields, Church Field, Heath Field and West Field. All the farmers had strips of land in each of those fields, originally based on the area that could be ploughed in a day - one acre.

In each of the fields it was required that the same crop was grown, wheat, barley, peas etc. or that the whole field was fallow. The pattern of ploughing caused a ridge and furrow undulation to the surface of the fields, with regions of build-up at the ends where plough soil was deposited over the centuries as the ploughs stopped, turned around, and went back again.

When our clerk with a ruler drew his line, his concern was tidiness and precision, not the existing field boundaries; his line dictated where a road would be created before tarmac was in common use and before earth levelling equipment was available. He therefore inadvertently preserved these ancient field headlands in every undulation in his ruler straight road.

But not every lump and bump is due to medieval farming practice.

CHAMPION AND WOODLAND LANDSCAPES

A glance at a map showing the area covering South Cambridgeshire and North Essex will show a quite dramatic change in the appearance of the countryside. The Cambridge section has villages with definite centres to them joined by long straight roads whilst just a few miles to the south it is difficult to pin point any village – just clusters of houses and farms standing in rather isolated positions with hedges surrounding. The roads tend to meander and are many and various. So what has happened to our countryside that caused these differences over such a short distance?

The accepted view is that we are seeing the boundary between the 'Planned Countryside' – that of Enclosure, and 'Ancient Countryside' of land that was never enclosed and still shows evidence of what England may have looked like at almost any time from the Bronze Age to the present. Other authors have given the name 'Champion' to the hedged countryside, perhaps derived from a 16th century poem that sings the praises of the hedges in the landscape. So the next time you travel from say Thriplow to Saffron Walden keep a good look out for an excellent example of the way the English landscape has evolved.

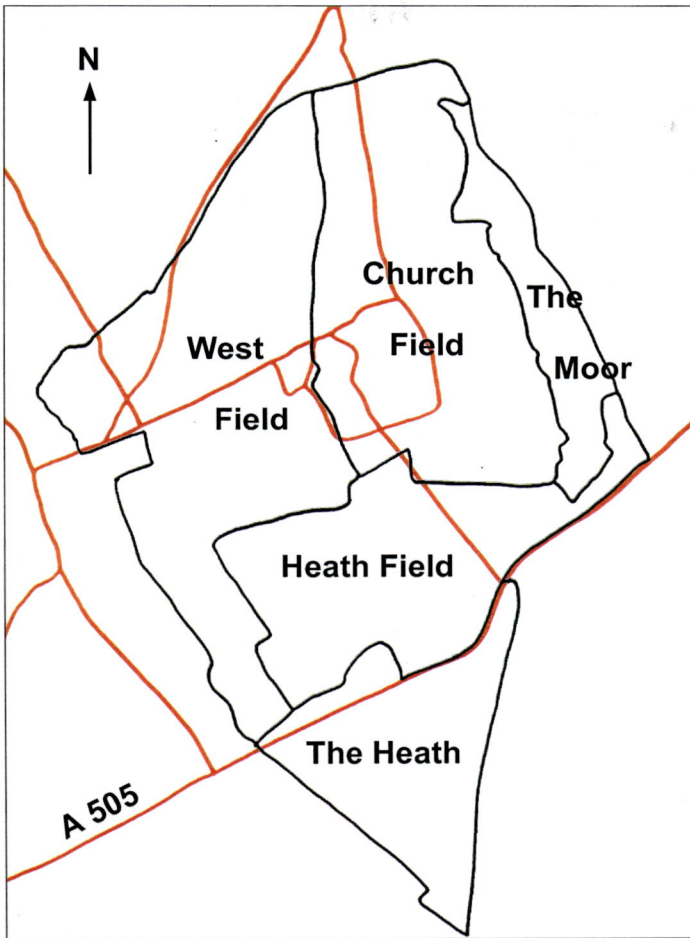

THE THREE FIELD SYSTEM

The three field system was a method of crop rotation widespread in the middle of England from the twelfth to the late eighteenth centuries. It comprised open fields divided into strips, so that each man had his fair share of crops.

Each village normally had three fields which were used for growing arable crops on a rotation basis. One field had strips growing grain, another growing pulses and one lay fallow for a year. The crops were rotated each year so that a different field lay fallow for the following year. These crops supplied the village with means of making bread, beer and fodder as required.

Each of these large fields was generally named from their location, for example, North Field, South Field etc. In Thriplow the three fields were called: West Field, Church Field and Heath Field.

Barley   Wheat   Peas

FARM ANIMALS IN THRIPLOW

Domesday Book records that in 1086 there were :
357 sheep
96 oxen
47 pigs
5 cattle
2 horses.

In a survey of 1279 :
960 sheep
30 pigs
1 boar
10 cows
1 bull.

The oxen were used to pull the ploughs and carts, horses were very expensive and only used by knights and high status people.

As can be seen the greatest number of farm animals were sheep. Thriplow and indeed the whole of south Cambridgeshire practised what is known as sheep-corn husbandry, this means that in the open fields that surrounded the village, sheep were led by a shepherd over the stubble and over the young corn. One field in three was left fallow to recover its fertility and the sheep and cattle were fenced in this field to feed on the weeds and fallen grain; in return their manure fertilized the land. On the fields with growing grain the sheep were folded using moveable hazel hurdles. Their small hooves acted as rollers to firm the light soil and they nibbled the growing shoots thus encouraging more shoots to grow, just like a grass mower. After a short time they were moved on. At other times they were kept on the Heaths. Right up to the advent of artificial fertilizers in the 19th century this was their most important role. The meat and wool although important were of a secondary value, though most cheese was made from sheep's' milk.

By the 16th century sheep had become so valuable that only Lords of Manors were allowed to keep them. The heath was divided up between the Lords, each of the four Lords and the Lessees' of the Rectory and Pittensaries owned a portion of the Heath. By the 18th century there were 1,400 sheep in the parish.

The cattle were also led out to pasture, each cow coming from its stall and joining the herd as it moved through the village and returning to its stall each evening. Cattle could also be led along the balks (grassy strips between the arable strips in the open fields) once the grain had been cut, and along the roadside verges. They were also tethered on the commons. There were strict rules about who could and could not keep cattle and other animals and how many and when they could be put on certain pieces of land. Fines were imposed if these 'stinting' rules were broken.

Before Enclosure the sheep would have been long legged and small, capable of walking many miles over the fields.

Another feature that you will notice is the modern speed bump protecting the village from those motorists who have just used a long straight road to explore the limits of the accelerator. Rest assured, they only do it once!

As you walk towards the A505, the land rises slightly and a scarp ridge becomes visible directly ahead and, at the highest point on the road, there is a small copse to the west. Surprisingly, the ridge, the road and the copse are all linked together in the local geology.

Having defined the course of a new road, the next step is to mark and build it. The marking would be accomplished with quickthorn hedges but the key feature of the road building was the surface. Luckily this area encompasses the possible route of an Ice Age river which concentrated gravel deposits, allowing them to be dug out of pits such as the one in the copse.

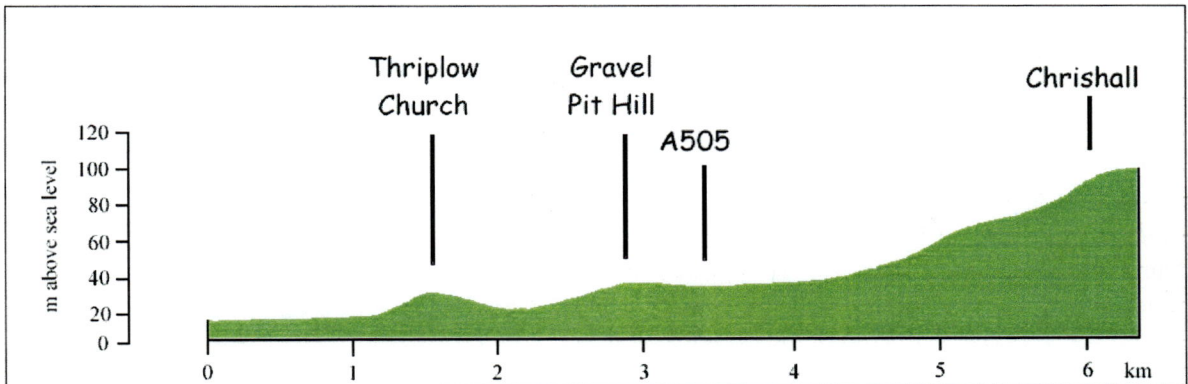

GRAVEL DEPOSITS

In the Anglian glaciation (or Great Ice Age) 450,000 years ago, glaciers dumped huge quantities of boulder clay (also known as till) and glacial gravels in the area. These deposits have been re-distributed by various methods, including torrential floods which occurred during thaws.

Gravels that have been deposited by rivers are termed River Gravels. During the Ice Ages, gravel near the surface in frozen sloping ground will gradually slip down slope if the surface is subject to freezing and thawing. This process is known as solifluction. The accumulation of such gravel at the bottom of a slope is termed Taele Gravel.

Determining the origin of gravel deposits can be difficult, since a variety of factors have caused a chaotic re-distribution of materials. The geology map designates areas of gravel in the south of Thriplow parish as Taele Gravels (that may have slipped down slope from the higher ground to the south). However a recent alternative theory suggests that they are river gravels deposited by a stream, which once ran aligned to the present A505, possibly incorporating some solifluction gravels.

More details are in the appendix.

Looking down on the A505 from this slight rise doesn't give you any feeling for the history of the place, it tends to make you contemplate the rise in dominance of the car and lorry. But look instead at the sweeping ridge ahead and imagine how a livestock trader from pre-car days to pre-history would have viewed it. In all probability something like 'I'm not taking this lot up that hill if I can help it!" That thought reoccurring through the ages gave us the Icknield Way, a broad swathe of trading route from central England to the Peddars Way and the Norfolk coast.

There are numerous tumuli lining the way, useful waymarkers when they were first made with a bright covering of chalk like a beacon. The easiest to see now from the main road or the train are just west of Royston, the rest have all but vanished under the plough.

The Victorians had a taste for investigating antiquities and in this area Richard Neville, who later became Lord Braybrooke, excavated many tumuli. We spent one long morning, with the help of the staff, retrieving his original records from the dusty recesses of the Cambridge University Museum of Archaeology and Anthropology.

The delicate watercolours of his finds and the accompanying notebooks record his disappointment at the lack of treasure to be found and give foundation to the modern arguments in archaeological circles over whether a site should be dug at all, or just left alone. The problem with the Victorian and later treasure hunter approach being that all the useful clues such as pollen or scraps of wood or leather are destroyed or discarded on the way.

Despite our efforts in searching out Richard Neville's original notebooks, which also included a visit to the Essex Records Office in Chelmsford, we were unable to locate precisely any of the tumuli he excavated. This gives you a good appreciation of the value of detailed and meticulous recording!

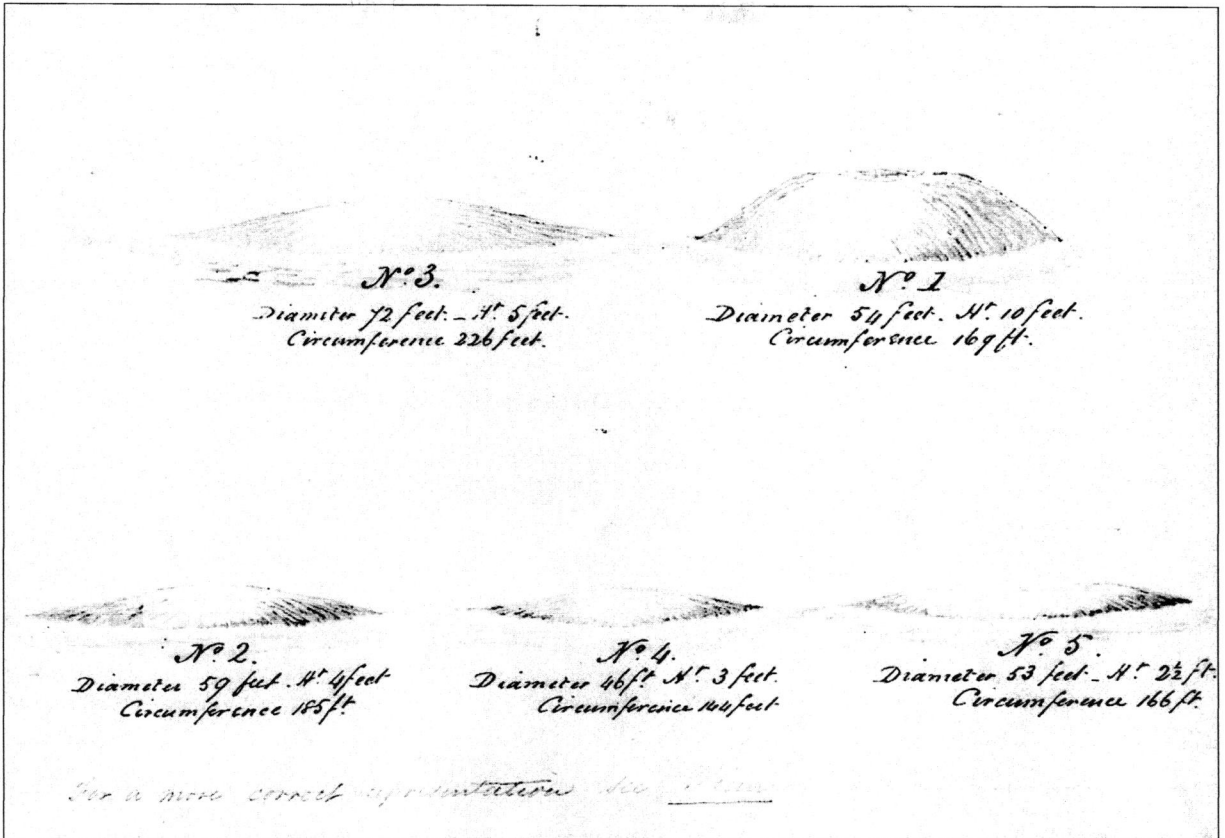

No. 3.
Diameter 72 feet. - Ht. 5 feet.
Circumference 226 feet.

No. 1.
Diameter 54 feet. Ht. 10 feet.
Circumference 169 ft.

No. 2.
Diameter 59 feet. Ht. 4 feet.
Circumference 185 ft.

No. 4.
Diameter 46 ft. Ht. 3 feet.
Circumference 144 feet.

No. 5.
Diameter 53 feet. Ht. 2½ ft.
Circumference 166 ft.

For a more correct representation see Plan

"Among the large enclosures which originally formed part of Thriplow Heath and have recently been completed stand a number of Tumuli of unequal distances and of irregular size......"

Extract and illustration from *Account of Some Barrows in Cambridgeshire* by the Hon. R.C.Neville FSA

A longer extract is in the appendix.

It wasn't always peaceful traders walking below the ridge, no doubt there were various military passages, at least sufficient to provoke the building during the fifth or sixth century of one of the series of ditches which stretch across Cambridgeshire. This one, Bran Ditch, starts in Heydon at the top of the ridge and drops down to the swampy ground at Fowlmere crossing the A505 at Flint Cross.

The only actual historical record of military interest was during the Civil War when the Parliamentarian Army camped in Heath Field whilst the townsfolk of Royston decided that a Royalist vote would not be a good idea! The aircraft hangers at Duxford and Fowlmere are monuments to much more recent military activity.

REMARKABLE EVENT IN THRIPLOW

It must have been a sight never seen before, or since, in Thriplow! On Thursday, June 10th 1647 20,000 men of Cromwell's army were reported to be camped on Thriplow Heath (the exact position is unclear but most likely was the area to the south of the present A505 road) awaiting instructions as there was concern over pay for the soldiers. The argument was apparently resolved and on the afternoon of the 10th the whole contingent moved on to camp at Royston.

Cromwell's soldiers sacking and burning in London.

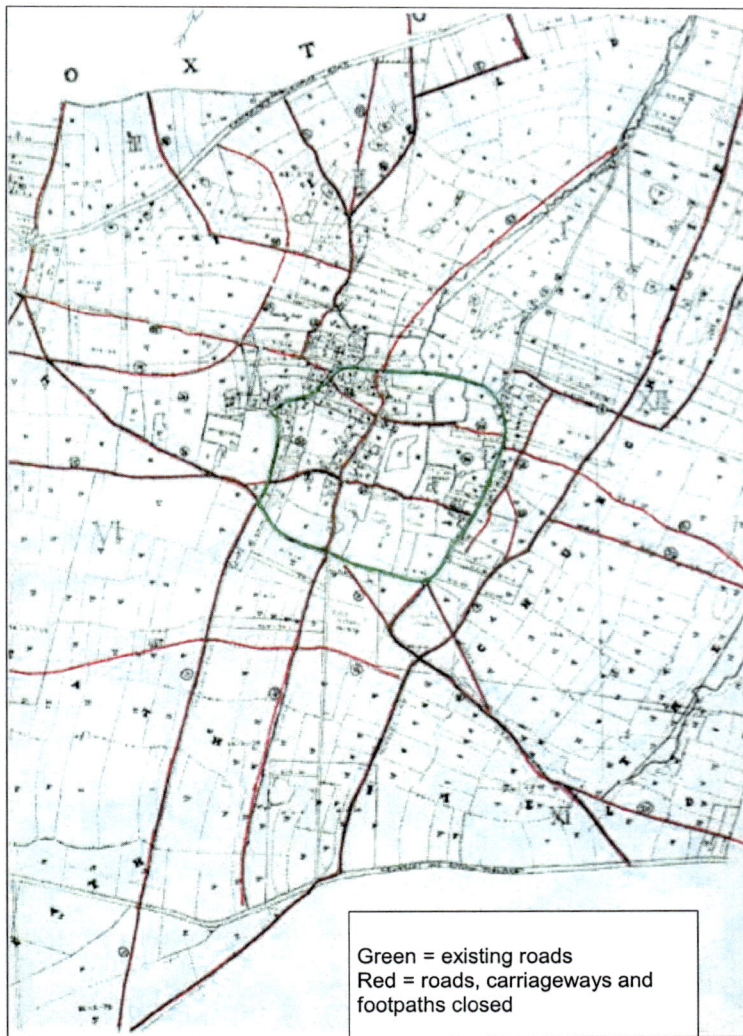

Green = existing roads
Red = roads, carriageways and footpaths closed

THE LOST ROADS OF THRIPLOW

When Thriplow was enclosed by Act of Parliament in 1840, many of the carriageways, bridleways and footpaths were stopped up. In fact there were 33 such paths. Notices were posted at both ends of such paths and details were printed in the local paper.

Many of these paths led to the cultivated strips within the open fields and therefore would no longer be needed once the land was allotted to individuals, but some led through the village to neighbouring villages and would have been useful. The enclosure commissioners allotted three footpaths for the use of the village and these three footpaths are now the only footpaths designated as such by the County Council.

There was no map showing the lost 33 paths and it took several of the Landscape Group many hours tracing them from the descriptions printed in the official notices which were displayed at the time.

TRAIL 7
UPPER GENTLEMAN'S FOOTPATH

Climb over the stile at the signposted start of the footpath in Church Street.

Bacon's Manor on your left, a former hall house, has chimneys dating from 1600. A ghost of a woman has been seen walking through a wall - which was discovered to have been a door.

Cross the field, go over the stile and then the bridge crossing the stream that hundreds of years ago was straightened to improve drainage.

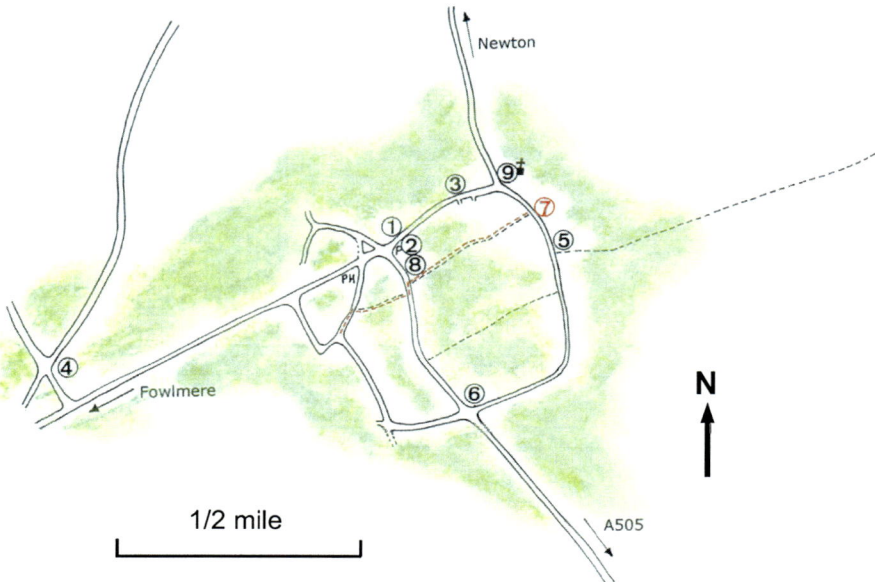

Newton

Fowlmere

N

1/2 mile

A505

Bacon's Manor

Turn left into Middle Street, then right at the sign. Go down the narrow lane known locally as Stinky Lane. Be careful not to fall down into the steep ditch beside you.

Look down over this low lying area of tussocky ground. Note that there are no buildings in this wet part of the village.

Interesting looking mounds in this field are still to be investigated and surveyed.

Further along notice the dovecote in the garden of Bassets, a beautiful jettied house. In Medieval times doves would have provided a welcome source of fresh protein in the winter.

At the end of the path in Lower Street notice the angled wall of the houses in front of you, Corkrane's.

Notice the octagonal brick chimney, typical of its time. These dwellings, originally one house, evolved from the late 16th century. When a later extension was added this had to take account of the bend in the road.

TRAIL 8
MIDDLE STREET

A small building in the garden of number 23 was built in 1834 at a cost of £40 as an independent chapel. In 1851 over 100 people attended, more than at the parish church.

Start at the new Village Hall.

Set back on your right stands a house with a steep roof, once thatched, and a medallion picture of George V on its wall. Pecks Close, the field next door, was left in 1633 by Francis Peck to provide an income for the poor. Until recently it was the village cricket ground.

Further down the road at Rectory Farm is the oldest secular building in Thriplow, the tithe barn dating from about 1320. Holes in the wall you see just before this building were air vents for a barn that no longer exists.

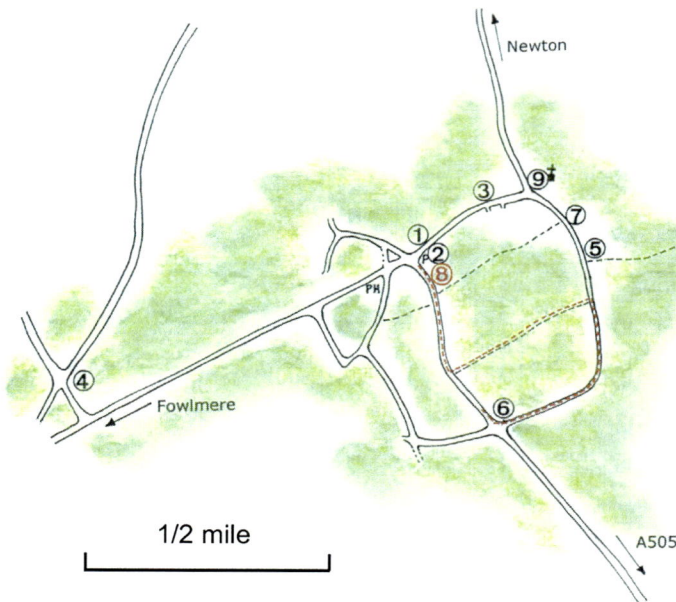

Newton

Fowlmere

1/2 mile

N

A505

Where the stream bends to the left springs can be seen in wet seasons.

Climb the stile and continue to the stile on the other side of the field.

Here on your right is "The View", an avenue of trees which led from the Newmarket Road (A505) to the manor on your left. Look through the gate and see the early 14th century moat.

Cross the footpath in the garden of Manor Farm, past another 15th century timber framed hall house.

The masters of St. John's college used Manor Farm as a refuge during times of plague.

Turn right into Church Street, follow the road along the South side of Thriplow noticing the open nature of the fields.

Just after turning right at the crossroads is an old chalk pit. At one time there was a lime kiln opposite.

TRAIL 9
THE CHURCH

Walk up the drive between a pantiled barn and an ivy covered flint wall to find Thriplow church set in a prominent position overlooking the village.

ANNO DOM 1687

The date you see on the wall of this thatched house indicates when the house was refurbished with a chimney and upper floor.

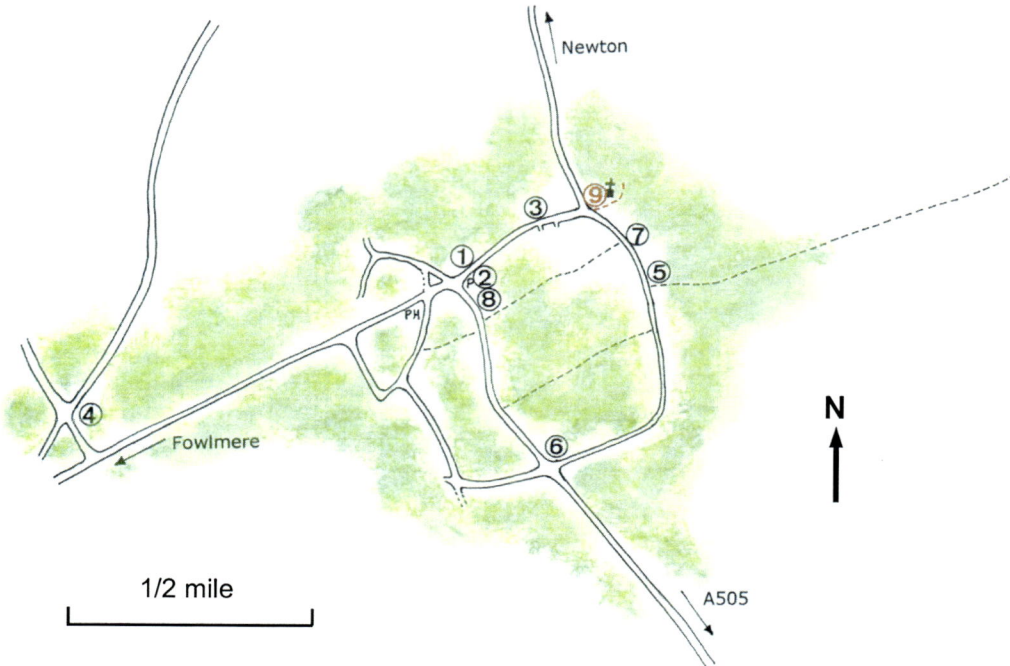

Newton

Fowlmere

A505

N

1/2 mile

Artist's impression of the East end of the village based on the 1886 Ordnance Survey map. The original painting by Shirley Wittering hangs in the village school.

Thriplow church drawn by William Cole in 1742

Thriplow church is just visible from the road.

Churches are the most characteristic feature of almost every English village. It used to be the church, the pub and the village shop but sadly the shops are succumbing to the supermarkets and pubs are suffering from the fierce taxation on alcohol amongst other problems. Amazingly, very little is known of the early life of the village church, basically because very few are demolished and the incumbents are understandably reluctant to allow archaeological digs in the grounds.

The first record of a church in Thriplow is in 1260, but it is almost certain that there was a church in the village well before this, because for promotion Saxon thegns needed to own four hides (about 500 acres) of land and a church, and Byrhtnoth, the Saxon landowner, was second in command to the Christian King Edgar in AD959. Byrhtnoth left the estates of Thriplow to the monks of Ely who took control in 1006 on the death of his wife Aelflead, both of which suggest he would have strongly favoured Christian churches in his holdings.

The earliest comprehensive record of England we all know as the 'Domesday Book'. Unfortunately, whilst this provides one picture of the countryside, it was done by William's version of the Inland Revenue who weren't about to tax the church, so they didn't need to record anything about it. Diocesan records give some clues but are largely concerned with land holdings and income rather than the churches themselves.

It is known that the early church favoured building on recognised pagan sites, so it could well be that St. George's which is at the extreme end of the present village, on its highest point, was deliberately built on top of a much earlier prominent burial mound.

It could be that a Saxon church in this position served a cluster of houses on the hill and that there were other churches within the area we now call Thriplow.

There was a rapid expansion in church building as the Normans became established but they sometimes built on new sites rather than on the old. We don't know, and won't know unless some excavation in the future just happens on an identifiable early church site. It is interesting that the church changed its name from All Hallows to St George's, which was first mentioned in 1851.

St George's is a lovely church to visit, with the odd surprise such as fragments of medieval wall painting and the array of spectacular hand sewn kneelers, totally overlooked until you retrace your steps from beneath the tower. The tower itself is a bit of a shock. Instead of the usual series of long wooden ladders giving precarious access to dark wooden platforms, or squeezing between the bell mountings, the interior has been refitted with industrial grade gantries and modern steps.

THRIPLOW CHURCH - WHAT TO SEE

The church is built from Barnack stone, flint and clunch so the most weathering will be on the clunch which is a basically chalk. There are some fragments of early Norman pillars in the north transept and a Norman font of Purbeck marble, which suggests that there was an earlier church here.

Inside there is a very interesting decorated rood screen, apparently used as a model for the one built in Great St Mary's Church in Cambridge in 1518. The rood screen dates from circa 1350 but sadly did not escape the attentions of the arch-vandal Dowsing in 1643. During its restoration in 1928 traces of ancient turquoise, gold, blue and red paint were uncovered on the base, perhaps all that was left of the 10 Commandments painted on the missing panels.

Further signs of the Dowsing visitation can be seen from the gravestones in the south transept with " ye brasses torn from them" according to Willaim Cole's inventory of 1742. Also in the south transept are the remains of an impressive canopied niche. These are just a few of the interesting things to be seen in this lovely old church

Medieval gargoyle and glass in the church.

One fine evening, by prior arrangement with the vicar, we had the rare treat of climbing to the top of the church tower. Luckily none of us suffer excessively from vertigo, but our group did seem to split between those hanging over the edge at the top, and those staying near the middle clutching the steeple! This could just have been worry at the very strong breeze which had cleared away the cloud and gave us fine views over the countryside.

Looking down towards the school we could easily see the ditch in the field behind and looking to the south we could see the boundaries and line of the cottages in Church street. These cottages are one of the strange features of the village, all with a common boundary at the back and to the road. All similar width plots, it's very much a planned development.

The thatched cottage at the junction gives us a date that could be near to the time this took place, or be very misleading - all we know is that the date relates to a rebuilding of the upper storey of that cottage. We also know that this type of planning took place in Ely, for example, before the Norman conquest.

View from the church tower looking South over the rooftops of Thriplow. The gentle chalk hills South of the A505 can be seen beyond.

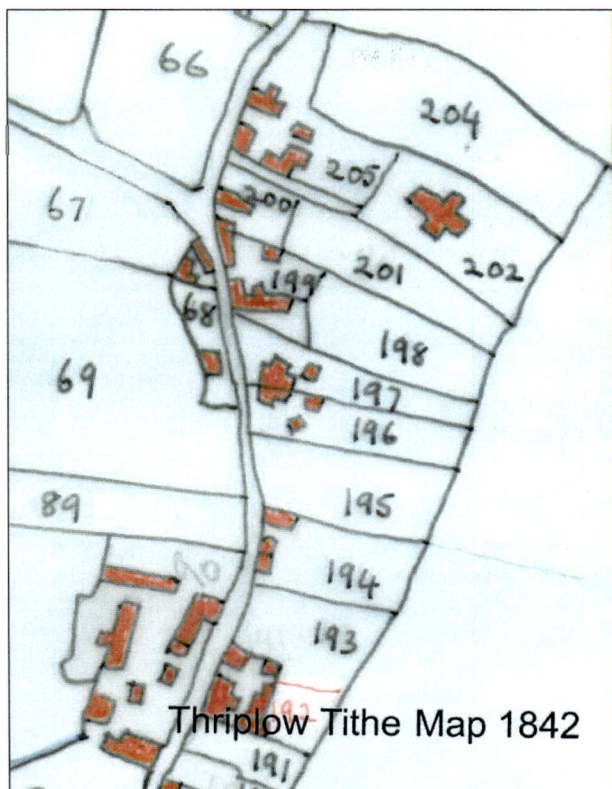

Thriplow Tithe Map 1842

The reason behind this planned development is unknown, likewise when it occurred. It may have been that several rainy years caused the land at the bottom of the slope to become too wet to live there, or that this seasonal pasture became too valuable for animal husbandry to waste the productive land on housing.

At Domesday the population of Thriplow was recorded as 27 workers, which with their families probably amounted to about 135 people. In 1327 the Subsidy Roll recorded 25 workers, amounting to about 125 people, but by 1664 the Hearth Tax survey recorded 245 people, an increase of about 50%.

See appendix article on Medieval climate.

Planned developments imply two basic concepts, firstly that someone was sufficiently in control to organise it, and secondly that some condition made it worthwhile to bother. The first may be assumed as the land has shown evidence of larger scale organisation from the Iron Age onwards, and by the 14th Century land holdings in Thriplow were well defined and divided amongst the church, the colleges of Cambridge and the manors of the village.

ALIGNMENTS OR LEYLINES

The mention of the word "leyline" to a group of "serious" archaeologists is likely to provoke an embarrassed silence or an attempt to change the subject, or both. This sometimes contentious term refers to alignments of ancient sites such as stone circles, standing stones, tumuli and early churches, together with natural features, especially hilltops. The existence of such alignments was first proposed by Alfred Watkins in the 1920s, and he coined the name "leylines". His classic book "The Old Straight Track" is now regarded as the Bible on this subject.

Watkins proposed that these tracks or leylines originated as a result of prehistoric man's desire to mark out the direction from one easily distinguishable site, typically a settlement, to another man-made feature or settlement many miles away, adopting the well proven principle of the shortest distance between two points is a straight line.

It would seem quite natural that many ordinary folk in prehistoric times would want to travel to neighbouring settlements to trade, or whatever, and would have appreciated a nicely waymarked route. Some of these sites may well have been regarded as "sacred" or become burial places for chieftains or other important people. In the Christian era, churches may have been built on these sites.

Perhaps inevitably, the concept of leylines has been rather hijacked by the von Daniken enthusiasts so that now these are sometimes associated with lines of force or mystical energy attracting the especial attention of aliens. Or perhaps aliens even caused them. Hence this topic has acquired a somewhat "fringe" reputation. This subject is more fully dealt with in the appendix, from which it may be seen that this subject cannot be so easily dismissed. Read it and make up your own mind!

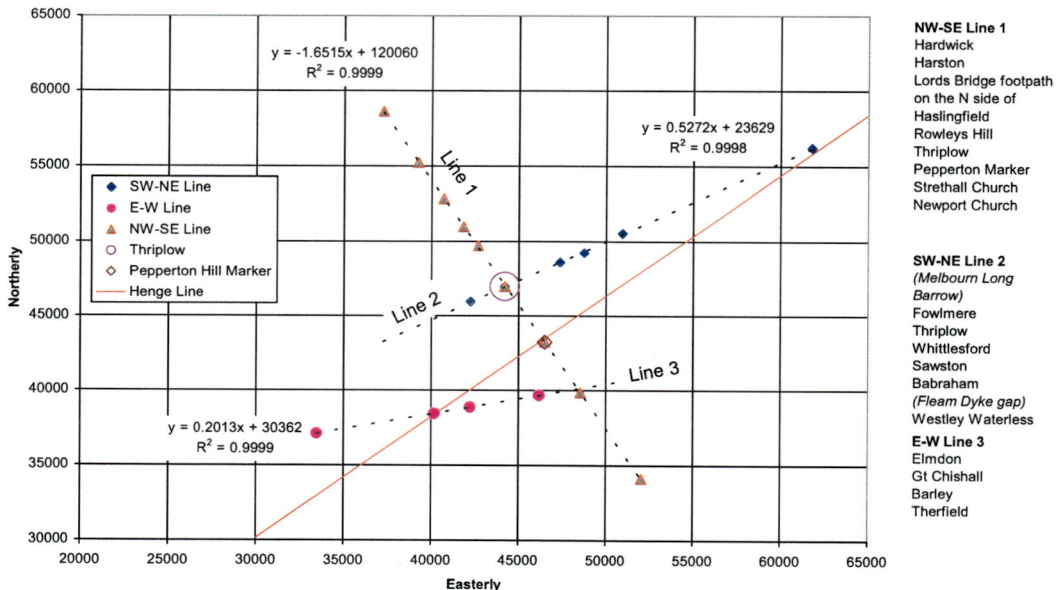

NW-SE Line 1
Hardwick
Harston
Lords Bridge footpath
on the N side of
Haslingfield
Rowleys Hill
Thriplow
Pepperton Marker
Strethall Church
Newport Church

SW-NE Line 2
(Melbourn Long
Barrow)
Fowlmere
Thriplow
Whittlesford
Sawston
Babraham
(Fleam Dyke gap)
Westley Waterless

E-W Line 3
Elmdon
Gt Chishall
Barley
Therfield

Our group, in addition to our common interest in landscape archaeology, encompasses a wide variety of other interests, not always wholly compatible. So it was that at a meeting one of our group in a pause said "I've been thinking about Leylines" - instant group polarisation! A load of rubbish or a well established idea.

Being open to new thoughts, we progressed to the problem of how you would establish any basis in fact that ancient monuments were in alignments. A few hours with a map and a long ruler suggested that several churches around Thriplow did indeed lie (or perhaps ley) in mainly two straight lines. The unresolved crunch came when we got to the point of how many churches in line make an alignment, closely followed by how near to a line do they have to be to count.

The latter point at least provided an excuse for an outing around the countryside visiting local churches with our GPS meter getting positions we could accurately plot. The question still remains though - when you have six churches that deviate from a line by only a few metres and certainly less than the length of the churches in question, were they deliberately constructed in a line?

It gets a bit more tricky when you move on to other ancient monuments or go to a greater distance when the curvature of the earth comes into play. However, we found it particularly thought provoking that a line joining Stonehenge and Arminghall henge near Norwich, running about a mile south of Thriplow church, passed as near as we could determine, straight through an isolated marker stone found on Pepperton Hill.

THE COUNTRYSIDE CODE

Be safe, plan ahead and follow any signs.

Leave gates and property as you find them.

Protect plants and animals, and take your litter home.

Keep dogs under close control.

Consider other people.

APPENDIX CONTENTS

APPENDIX

DOCUMENTS AND RECORDS RELATING TO THRIPLOW

DOMESDAY 1068 including the two versions relevant to the diocese of Ely Inquisito Eliensis and Inquisito Comitatus Cantabrigiensis. These last two include items such as the number of animals that are not mentioned in the Domesday Book.

ROTULI HUNDREDORUM or the Hundred Rolls of 1279, translated from the latin by Shirley Wittering. This survey of Thriplow is much fuller than DB and covers everyone in the parish, their land and labour services.

MANOR COURT ROLLS of the 4 manors in Thriplow -
The Bury from 1587
Barringtons Manor from 1640 and terriers from 1617
Bacons Manor from 1561 and terriers from 1612
Crouchmans from 1704 and terriers from 1537
A further terrier or survey for Pittansaries dates from 1649 and mentions the Guildhall.

WILLS & INVENTORIES from 1471 with a database of names and properties.

LAND LEASES & RELEASES

LAY SUBSIDIES 1327, 1379, 1523, 1546, 1640, 1645

HEARTH TAX 1662, 1664, 1666, 1674

FREE GIFT 1661

REGISTERS (Transcripts) Baptisms from 1538, Marriages from 1599, Burials from 1600

NONCONFORMITY, there are many records on this subject.

C of E SCHOOL REGISTERS from 1864, LOG BOOKS from 1864

OVERSEERS' ACCOUNTS from 1764, includes lists of names

CHURCHWARDENS' ACCOUNTS from 1637, & names

MAPS from OS draft 1799 & 1810

INCLOSURE AWARD & MAP 1840, includes list of closed roads which have been traced and mapped.

TITHE MAP & names 1842

LAND TAX, 1703, 1778, 1818-1865, 1836

POOR RATE, 1836

PHOTOGRAPHIC RECORD of old Thriplow

APPRENTICESHIPS AND EMIGRATION lists, incomplete.

POPULATION NUMBERS

Records from PETERHOUSE COLLEGE

FIELD BOOK 1780

Records from ST JOHN'S COLLEGE incomplete

THRIPLOW'S HISTORY FROM DOCUMENTS

Liber Ramsiensis and Liber Eliensis:
From these we learn the story of Earldorman Bryhtnoth who bequeathed his estate in Thriplow to the Abbot of Ely in his will. Bryhtnoth was brought up in the household of King Athelstan and became second in command to his son, Edmund. He was killed fighting the Danes at the battle of Maldon in 991. He owned much land in Cambridgeshire which on his death became the property of the monks of Ely.

Domesday Book:
Inquisitio Eliensis was probably made for Ely, Inquitsitio Comitatus Cantabrigiensis was the original version and the third was the final copy. Thriplow at this time had two manors, the Bury (meaning a fortified dwelling) which belonged to the Bishop of Ely, and Barenton's; both these manors have moats. Domesday shows that Thriplow had a population of approximately 135 people.

Hearth Tax:
People owning property worth less than twenty shillings a year were exempt. Most of these returns have survived and give lists of inhabitants and numbers of hearths. The population by this time was around 200 less than in 1279; the Black Death and following plagues probably accounts for this drop. There is further information in the appendix article on Medieval climate.

Registers:
Baptisms from 1538, Marriages from 1599 and Burials from 1600:
There is an interesting entry for the year 1650, recording the marriage of Dr Thomas Bakenham of Cambridge University with Mary Birchmore of Thriplow. Members of the University at this time were not allowed to marry, but some sneaked off to a nearby village to marry clandestinely.

HUNDRED ROLLS-1279

The population had now risen to 440. Surnames at this time were still personal, describing a person's occupation, (cook), dwelling place (at wood) or some physical feature (red head). Some of the names in the Hundred Rolls are still names of fields and landscape features in Thriplow today; Godson's Grove and Squirrel's Close where we did some of our earliest surveying both refer to people mentioned in this document.

By the fourteenth century documents were appearing which mentioned names which were to become further manors - Bacon's and Crouchman's.

Opposite is a transcript from the printed version made by the Royal Commission for Ancient Manuscripts between 1808 and 1818.

This document inquires where and what is held by anyone, Bishop,

Abbot, Prior, Earl, Baron, Knight and Free men.etc.

We declare the Bishop of Ely hold in the town of Trippelowe as

tenant in chief of the Lord King 18 score (360) acres of arable land

with manor and garden containing 2 acres and of pasture 5 acres

and 1 rood and of separate pasture 45 acres.

The Bishop also has 1 windmill and has gallows and tumbrel,

assise of bread and ale and view of frankpledge, return of writs

and all that pertains to justice and free warren but without knowing

by whose warrant and the said Bishop has the said advoweson of

the church but it is not known by whose warrant.

THRIPLOW RECKONING COUNTER

This is a reckoning or casting counter. It was used on a reckoning board or cloth for doing accounts in Roman numerals. When schoolmasters taught children how to 'caste accomptes' they were teaching them how to lay out the counters to add and subtract (both quick and easy), multiply (more complicated) and divide (quite horrible) without the benefit of arabic (really Indian) numerals.

From the thirteenth century onwards the Italians used arabic numerals, which gave them an advantage over north Europeans who went on using counters until the seventeenth century. Rich men and government officials had special sets of counters made for them, often in silver. Most people used brass counters. In the fifteenth century they were mostly made in the Meuse valley around Liege, in the sixteenth in Nuremberg.

The two most important manufacturers in Nuremberg in the second half of the sixteenth century were the Schultes and the Krauwinckel families. They sold them in immense numbers not only in Germany, but also in France and particularly the Netherlands (with their own salerooms in Paris and Antwerp) and through Antwerp into England. They were sold in sets (I think of a hundred counters) in little boxes. In the first half of the seventeenth century the use of arabic numbers and arithmetic on paper took over in English schools and by the second half of the century only a few elderly people were still using counters. When they were lost people did not worry much. When they were not used any more, they were thrown away. Lots have been found in London rubbish pits.

This particular one we found in Thriplow:

Obverse. Imperial orb in a complicated three lobed double pattern with pointed corners and annulets in between the corners. This is derived from the normal design on imperial gold gulden from the fifteenth century onwards. [the fifteenth century Liege counters also copied the designs of gold coins]. The Orb held by the Emperor at his coronation went with Imperial claims to universal dominion, the orb representing the world, with a cross on it. In German the orb was nicknamed the Reichsapfel, the imperial apple, and so these counters were popularly known in German as 'Apfelpfennige', apple pennies. Around the orb is the name of the manufacturer: HANS SCHLLTES NOR le. Hans Schultes of Nor(imberg), Nuremberg. Unfortunately there were three generations of men called Hans Schultes, and it is not easy to tell which is which. Hans Schultes I, was the son of Jörg Schultes, admitted a **Master in his guild 1553, died 1584; Hans** II was the son of **Hans** I, died 1603; **Hans** III **was the** son of Hans II, **no documentary references after 1612.** Theoretically it could be any one of them, and made between 1553 and 1612 (or even later). However Wolfgang Hess has divided them on stylistic grounds into four types and this is Type 3. If he has the order right, I would guess it was probably Hans II or III. In the Hess catalogue it is no. 518.

Reverse. In the centre a 6 leaved rosette, surrounded by 3 crowns and 3 lilies, the whole surrounded by a wreath of leaves with rosettes at top and bottom. The wreath was instead of an inscription. The inscriptions sometimes repeated the name of the maker Hans Schultes, they were sometimes pious sentiments in either German or Latin (for sale at home or abroad) like *Gotes wort bieibt ewig* or *Verbum Domini manet in aeternurn* (God's word endures for ever) or popular sayings *Glück is faisch und flütchtig* (Fortune is false and fleeting).

We thank Professor Spufford for his help with this section.

THE MEDIEVAL CLIMATE OF THRIPLOW AND ITS EFFECT ON THE LOCAL POPULATION

The climate has probably played a greater role in the development of Thriplow into a modern village than in many other South Cambridgeshire villages because it has numerous springs, which give rise to the "soggy ground" in the geographical centre of Thriplow and the water meadows to the west and south-west of the church.

It is probable, in a relatively warm and not too wet climate, that settlements were created near to these springs. The Thriplow Landscape Research Group has found evidence of such settlements, surviving as some humps around a distinct hollow-way just to the north of School Lane opposite Middle Street (map ref. 437468), and 0.5 Km to the north-east (map ref 440469) the remains of a moat, with the Church being the dominant feature about 200m further East. The positioning of these two sites can be seen from the map indicated as A and B. Many springs erupt in the darker shaded area in the centre of Thriplow where it is characteristically muddy in wet weather, and even in not so wet conditions. It is perhaps significant that these two sites are on the line of the ancient Ashwell Street which may have been a northern branch of the Icknield Way. Some pottery was recently found at site B and authoritatively dated to be not later than the 13th century. This is significant in view of the following evidence of severe climate changes between 1300-1325 AD and its effect on the population of Thriplow.

While, unsurprisingly, there is relatively little direct recorded evidence of the climate trends during the period of from 1000 AD to about 1400 AD, there has been quite considerable research into the climate of East Anglia. Much can be deduced from the effect of climate on the growth of crops, as can often be gleaned from the records of Manorial courts as reported by Petty, Newman and Harvey provide evidence that the wheat harvest at Cuxham in Oxfordshire declined by 25% from 1300 to 1350 AD. This indicates that there was a severe constraint affecting harvests during this time, when an increase might have been expected, or at least a steady state. The authors suggest that this was primarily due to a decline in soil fertility as a result of decreasing levels of phosphorus in the soil, as this was not being replaced naturally by cattle. It is possible that this was caused by over exploitation of the land, which was then insufficiently fertilized by cattle and sheep. This may not necessarily have been as a direct result of climate change, but it is likely that the climate changes described below may have been a contributory factor.

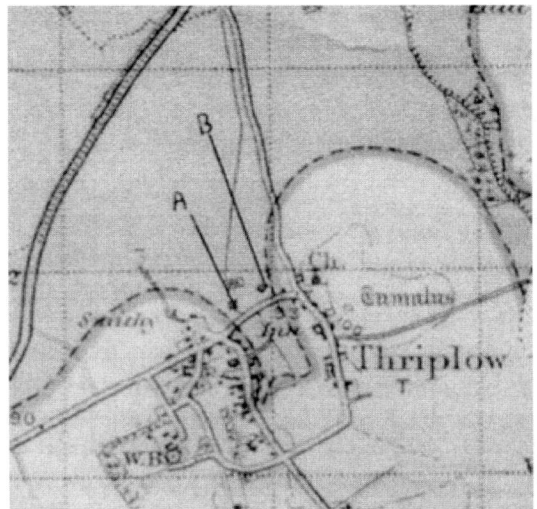

One relevant contemporary written record from the Calendar of Patent Rolls at the Cambridge Record Office, provided by Shirley Wittering, is reproduced below:

10th April. Edward III (1336)
Commission to Simon de Brunne and Geoffrey Seman Waltham
Inquisition- Cambridge Saturday before St Dunstan
The growing corn of the men of Fulbourne, Badburgham, Wytlesford, Dokesworth, Pampesworth and Sauston totally perished in a sudden storm of hail and rain on Sunday before St Peter's Chains last, so that they completely lost the corn with the straw and forage, and nothing remained for the maintenance of themselves and their servants except what they could obtain by loan.
In Litle Abyton all the corn perished, the men of Babham, Trippelowe and Great Abonton lost half their corn with the straw and forage: the men of Stapilford and Hildresham a third: and the men of Wrattyng, Weston, Great and little Wilburgham, Ikelyton and Hynxston a forth.

NB. The feast of St Peter's Chains, *St Peter and Vincula,* is August 1st. In 1335 the Sunday before this fell on July 28th.

There is a curious inconsistency in this record, or is there a distinction between the growing corn which was totally lost in Badburgham, and the corn of Babham of which only half was lost? Can it be assumed that the two places are one and the same, the result of clerical misspelling which was obviously very common. Perhaps the more likely explanation is that "Babham" is simply a misspelling of Balsham.

H. Hallam studied local records of harvests of barley, wheat and oats and compared them with contemporary accounts of the weather in E England between 1250 and 1350 and presents a table showing the weather, harvests and agrarian crises in E England during this time. The harvests from 1272 to 1288 were cited as being good/ very good although there were numerous summer droughts during this time. From 1289 until 1326 there were numerous harvests described as "poor" to "abysmally poor", with the severest failures occurring between 1315 until 1321, all of which were described as famine years. Hallam does, however, indicate that considerable caution needs to be exercised in interpreting these findings as these reported famines were by no means universal, although it does appear that generally this period was pretty dreadful for most of the rural community.

The common factor contributing to these famines was wet autumns which ruined the harvests. However, Hallam also presents a table showing just the records of barley harvests during this time which appeared to be relatively little affected by the adverse growing conditions between 1315-1321. Since barley was a predominant crop in E England it may be surmised that the famines may not necessarily have been universal and it is possible, but from the population figures given below, not probable, that the rural medieval population of Thriplow may have been spared this famine. However, the dramatic pre Black Death population decline of Thriplow may well have been the result of much of the settled land becoming uninhabitable as a result of the heavy rainfalls noted from 1315-1322.

The late H.H. Lamb, a leading climatologist who founded the world renowned Climatic Research Unit at the University of East Anglia, in his "Climatic History and the Modern World" presents graphical estimates of the temperature changes in central England between 800-1900 AD. This shows that the temperatures reached a maximum at around 1200 AD but then declined very sharply, especially the midsummer temperatures. Significantly the summer rainfall increased dramatically in the 1310s and this, combined with the drop in temperatures made for increasingly cold and wet summers from around 1300 AD onward. Lamb suggests that England experienced mostly warm, dry summers from 1284 until 1314. This was then followed by an "extraordinary run of wet summers and mostly wet springs and autumns with 1315 being the worst year with famine in many parts of Europe... "great numbers of sheep and cattle died in the epidemics which swept the sodden and often flooded landscape".

This picture appears to be reinforced by the dendrochronological evidence obtained from oaks at Chicksands Priory, obtained by Howard et al, from Nottingham University.

The Tree Ring Width Chart in Trail 1 shows the 5 yearly average tree ring widths from 1200 to 1400.

This needs to be interpreted with some caution and the late Tony Carter, an historical climatologist at the Cambridge University Godwin Institute, suggested that the first 30 years may be ignored as the early tree-ring growth patterns are rarely representative. We thus see a fairly steady 1.1-1.4mm average from 1230 until 1270, reducing to an average of 1mm between 1270 -1295, then sharply down to 0.7mm between 1300 to 1330, followed by a recovery up to 1mm from 1330 until 1350. While it is rather difficult to correlate fully this dendrochronological data with climate, the low tree ring widths from 1300 to 1325 correlates remarkably well with the climate evidence already discussed and also presented by Ogilvie and Farmer. A block diagram shows the 1310s having both severe winters and excessive summer wetness, again reinforcing the impression that this was not the ideal climate to be living on low lying land adjacent to springs. It is perhaps significant that the name of

School Lane in the early 19th century was Gutter Lane. In prolonged wet conditions it could well have looked like one!

Paul Simons in "Weird Weather" writes: " from parish and tax records, the population fell to one third between 1300 -1327 (more than by the Black Death) as a result of long harsh winters, late springtimes, poor harvests and ergot poisoning .... Boglands grew in the cold, wet climate and forced many populations out of valley bottoms which were becoming increasingly flooded. Maybe one-half of the population of Britain was wiped out in the appalling climate". This would seem to imply, after taking the Black Death into consideration, that the immediate post Black Death population was less than one quarter of that in 1300. The following population figures of Thriplow (kindly supplied by Shirley Wittering) would appear to indicate that this assertion may possibly have some credence, certainly as far as Thriplow is concerned.

DATE SOURCE
ESTIMATED POPULATION

Date	Source	Estimated Population
1068	DOMESDAY	135
1279	HUNDRED ROLLS	430
1327	LAY SUBSIDY*	125
1523	LAY SUBSIDY*	260
1662	HEARTH TAX *	245

*Tax payers only. These figures have been multiplied by 5 as only heads of households were counted.

What this shows is that the low population figure in 1327 occurred AFTER the appalling weather between 1315-23 but BEFORE the Black Death in 1349! This poses the intriguing possibility that perhaps the commonly held view that the Black Death was responsible for a 30 to 50% decline in the population in the mid 14th century may be partially as a result of the Black Death fatalities being merged with the population decline in the 1320s. The relative paucity of population data at this time may have tempted some researchers to make assumptions that the documented population differences between the late 13th century and after 1350 were entirely attributable to the Black Death. Many historians believe that the Black Death was a culmination of many years of poor fertility, famine and disease aggravated by the cold and wet weather. However, the dendrochronlogical and climatic evidence presented here suggests that the weather improved from 1325 onwards allowing for a recovery period of 25 years, or one generation, until the intervention of the Black Death. This would favour the scenario of two separate 14th century population catastrophes.

There is some evidence, provided by Rowland Parker that the neighbouring village of Foxton, some 3 km to the north-west did not suffer the same drastic depopulation in the 1310s as appeared to happen in Thriplow, suggested by the fourth rebuilding of Foxton Church occurring between 1318-1328. Surely this is unlikely to have occurred had Foxton been suffering from the same severe pre Black Death depopulation as it appears was happening in Thriplow during this time.

This suggests that this pre Black Death depopulation was NOT a nationwide phenomenon, but only experienced in villages sensitive to extremely wet weather such as Thriplow. In other words, it seems that Thriplow experienced what might be called a "double whammy" of two severe population declines in the 14th century.

It is necessary to make the caveat that these population figures may not necessarily be comparable or accurate, but they do indicate a fascinating area for further research where my interpretations may, or may not, be confirmed!

We might therefore surmise that the severe population decline in Thriplow between 1279 to 1327 is attributable to much of the previously inhabited parts of Thriplow becoming uninhabitable as a result of the heavy rains in the 1310s, resulting in the above mentioned "soggy ground" syndrome. But however these population figures are interpreted, they show a truly catastrophic population decline in Thriplow from the heady days of the 1280s. It is thus probable that these settlements were abandoned because of the severe wet weather between 1315 –1327, never to be resettled whilst the people living on the higher, but less fertile ground, by the Church in Church Street were relatively unaffected so did not need to abandon their houses.

SOIL RESISTIVITY TECHNIQUES

The systematic measurement of the soil resistance at frequent intervals can provide the archaeologist with valuable information on what is buried underneath the soil. Because soil contains water—soluble, ionisable minerals such as salt, then especially when damp, it will be measurably conducting, so will have a relatively low electrical resistance compared with bricks, stones, slabs, etc. which do not contain any water—soluble minerals. Man-made features that can give low resistance are backfilled trenches and graves. On a slightly macabre note, the latter will result in a concentration of water soluble salts, which, of course, are conductive in moist soil resulting in a relatively low soil resistance measurement.

To carry out a systematic sequence of soil resistance measurements it is first necessary to set out a grid carefully so that you know exactly where changes in resistance are occurring. This is usually a 20m x 20m square, subdivided into 0.5 m or, more usually, 1 m squares covering an area in which signs of man's past activity is being investigated. To get a complete picture it is usually necessary to carry out a soil resistance survey of several such grids, each carefully measured out relative to the baseline of the first grid or some convenient fixed point such as a tree or fence post.

The equipment, usually in what is known as the twin probe configuration, is shown in the diagram. It comprises two transmitter probes, T1 and T2, two receiver probes, R1 and R2, a meter box and connecting cables. The meter box and probes R1 and T1, the mobile probes, are fixed to a frame so that the mobile probes are spaced 50 cm apart. The other pair, the remote probes, are put into the ground at least 15 metres away from any part of the grid and at approximately 1 metre apart. They remain fixed while the survey over the grids is made.

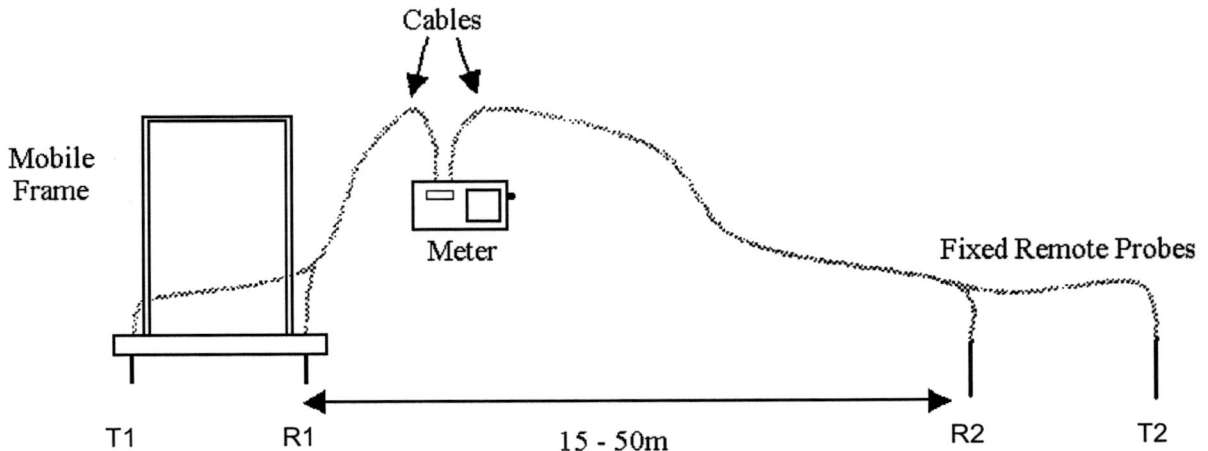

Cables

Mobile Frame

Meter

Fixed Remote Probes

T1   R1   15 - 50m   R2   T2

The resistance when a current flows between the probe R1 inserted in a grid square and the probe R2 at the remote position can then be found. A current I from a constant current source transmitter in the meter box flows between the two transmitter probes, and the voltage V is measured between the two receiver probes, R1 and R2. The resistance R can then be calculated using Ohm's Law R=V/I, displayed on the meter and recorded. This arrangement is used to ensure the underground resistance is measured rather than the resistance between the soil and the probe surface, known as the contact resistance, which can be very high and is irrelevant to what we wish to measure.

To collect resistance values over the grid, the mobile probes are inserted into each square of the grid in turn as the operator walks up and down the lines of the grid. If the mobile probes encounter an area with boulders or bricks, higher resistance will be recorded. If the mobile probes penetrate a region which was once a pit, this will probably be damper relative to the surrounding soil and a lower resistance value will be expected. The data obtained is in the form of resistance values. When the data is automatically stored into a data logger, 400 readings at 1m intervals in a typical 20m^2 grid can be carried out very quickly.

Since the maximum depth of measurement is reckoned to be about 1.5x the mobile electrode separation, a 1m electrode separation will enable anomalies of down to 1.5m to be detected, which, in archaeological terms is very deep. However, the greater the electrode separation, the poorer the discrimination which may lead to smaller anomalies not being detected. Ergonomically, a 0.5m electrode separation is near optimal for most users whereas a probe with an electrode separation of 1m would be unwieldy. For better discrimination, readings might be taken at shorter intervals such as every 0.5m in a 20m^2 grid but this would entail many more readings. Because of these considerations, a frame with an electrode separation of 0.5m, with readings every metre, is usually employed

Fortunately, with the advent of "easy to use" clever software and relatively inexpensive computers, all the number crunching can be done very quickly so really all that is required is a degree of accuracy and a systematic technique to make a suitable grid for meaningful measurements to be carried out.

With suitable software a diagrammatic plot of regions of high and low resistance can be displayed. Variations could be caused by geological conditions or buried pipes etc, or it could show evidence of man's activity beneath the soil as can be seen from a recent resistance survey of the Thriplow tumulus site, about 200m south-east of the Church. Evidence of the original ring, no longer visible from the surface, can be seen very clearly. Darker squares show a low relative resistance and lighter squares a high resistance. The darker ring shows the in-filled ditch around the tumulus. This correlates remarkably well with Dr Trump's plan (indicated by the red hatching) which he made following his excavations at this site in 1953.

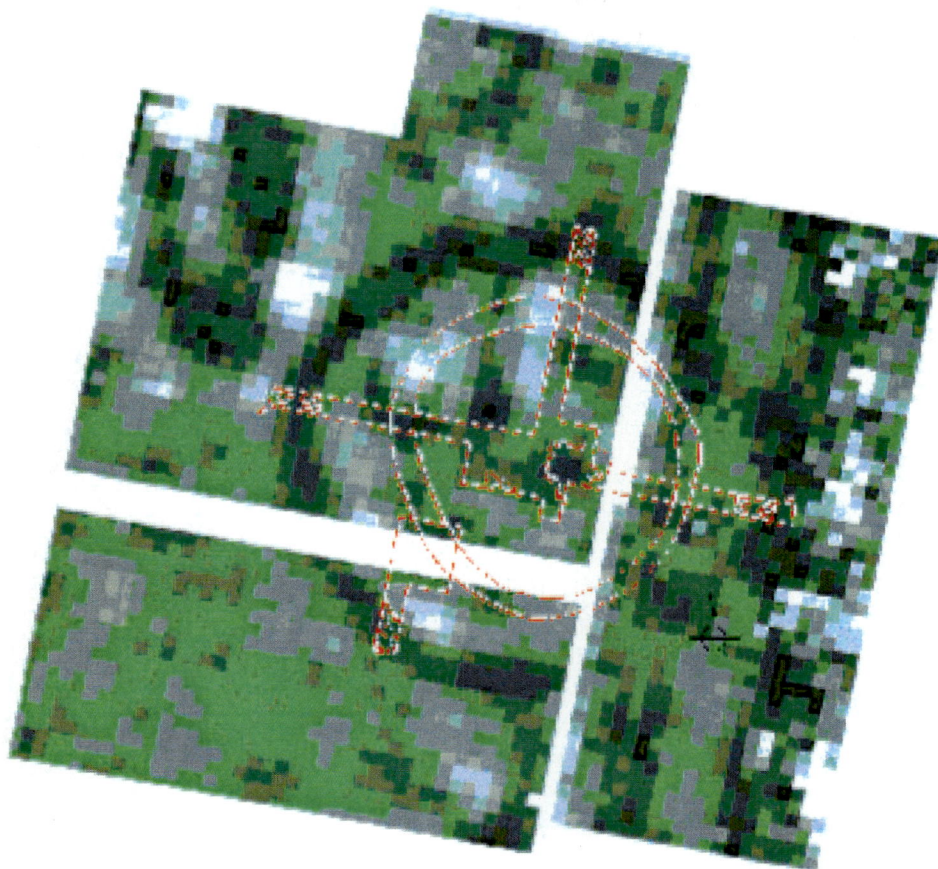

The Thriplow Landscape Research Group presented this overlay of resistance data and site survey to David Trump in September 2003, 50 years after his excavation in 1953.

The image shows the resistance measured in the soil as coloured squares where different colours represent different resistance values. The straight red lines show where excavations were carried out in 1953. The red circles show where the chalk facing of the tumulus was probably located.

The shading at the ends of the excavation trenches indicate where evidence of the outer ditch was discovered and coincides with the dark green circle of the resistance data. This clearly shows that the ditch continues all the way around the barrow. The white areas represent fences which prevented the collection of resistance data. The dark green in the centre of the circles is probably due to the original excavation.

ACCOUNT OF SOME BARROWS IN TRIPLOW IN CAMBRIDGESHIRE
By the Hon. R.C.Neville FSA

Among the large enclosures which originally formed part of Triplow Heath & have recently been completed stand a number of Tumuli of unequal distances and of irregular size – Tradition has assigned them (for as far as I can learn they have never been examined scientifically or by the curious) to the Anglo-Saxons – From their appearance I was anxious to obtain leave to open them and the following is the account of one of the smallest which I have just examined by permission of Mr Perkins – I commenced operations with 4 men on Wednesday July 29th by driving a shaft Horizontally thro' the centre 6 feet in width and about 8 Inches below the level of the original surface. This was completed July 30th . Year 1846 see ' Sepulchre Exposita' P.3.13.

The first thing that presented itself worthy of notice was a small fragment of black Pottery apparently part of a Vase; which from its similarity in texture and marking to one found under the same circumstances in Suffolk, I judge to be Anglo-Saxon. Next one jaw bone of a Horse and on reaching the exact centre, a very perfect skull with other human bones and the remaining jaw bone of the Horse; all the pottery was completely burnt thro' as well as the Human bones earth bearing evident marks of fire, but exhibiting no remains of importance, except a curious skewer shaped implement of bone – I then gave directions for making a traverse cutting 23ft in Diameter, 3ft 2in deep in the centre – but nothing further was elicited by it: in filling in however, we found a very poor Coin, evidently Roman and proving to be of the Emperor Valentinian the first – It is the opinion of E.Jones Esq. Surgeon that the skull already referred to, is that of a fine Young Male, in the Prime of Life (probably a Saxon Warrior) and we may also infer from the healthy appearance and good preservation of the teeth, that he came to a sudden and violent death, or at least was not the victim of disease.

On the completion of this excavation July 31st I attacked a Barrow of much larger dimensions and greater importance, not far from the proceeding one. The report goes that two swords were taken from it at no distant period, in working superficially and merely for Agricultural purposes; I naturally therefore hoped for a good result

in going deeper, but encountered only burnt bones, earth and pottery in a small quantity – This Barrow is longer than broad and the cutting ran straight thro' the centre – which proving totally devoid of curious matter, I determined August 3rd to turn the earth completely over, in order, to make sure that nothing escaped me; as it was hardly probably that so large a Mound would have been raised without some definite object. This fresh research was only rewarded by finding the bottom of a bottle in very thick glass (of a deeper colour and yet more solid material than that discovered in the Bartlow Hills and at Chesterford) and a bone pronounced by the Faculty to have appertained to a Cow – Discouraged by these failures, I only removed half of the Barrow .

Museum of Archaeology and Anthropology
Box 3 GO2/2/1

THRIPLOW CHURCH

Thriplow Church, the Church of St George or All Saints, to give its full title, is a fine cruciform shaped building with its origins dating back to the early 12th century. It may be significant that this is only about 200m to the north-west of the burial tumuli (or low) of the Bronze Age chieftain believed to be called Trippa, hence Trippa's Low.

Curiously, the very interesting monograph on the church by Geoffrey Vinter records the legend that the original location of the Church was intended to be in the meadow near to the Townsend Springs, behind the school, but the " the Devil came and tore up the foundations". Perhaps a more likely explanation would be the probable frequent flooding of that area which would have made a mess of any foundations. The Church was involved in the establishment of the University in Cambridge through the Bishop of Ely, Hugh de Balsham who in 1284 used the Church tithes to found Peterhouse, the first college.

The church has at least 4 recorded cases of its being used as a place of sanctuary in the 13th century. Those accused of capital offences, on seeking sanctuary were allowed the stark choice of submitting to justice (and, inevitably, a noose suspended sentence) or "abjuring the Realm", requiring the applicant immediately to leave the country by boat, "unshod, in his bare shirt", from the nearest port.

Far from seeking sanctuary, the most destructive and odious visitor to the Church was the prince of iconoclasts, the Puritan William Dowsing who "visited" Thriplow Church in 1643. He wrote in his Journal "we brake about 100 Cherubins and superstitious pictures (which included stained glass windows).... and to level the steps". While most of his vandalism was restored by the 19th century some traces can still be found.

This is just a taste of the fascinating history of this Church from the era of the Saxon nobleman Byrhtnoth, killed by the Danes at the Battle of Malden in 990, to the present Daffodil Week-end.

LEYLINES OR ALIGNMENTS CENTERED ON OR NEAR TO THRIPLOW

As mentioned in Trail 9, the investigation of leylines was NOT on the original research agenda until one of the members suggested to a then sceptical group the existence of TWO possible alignments passing through Thriplow, avoiding the term "Leylines" for fear of incurring even greater scepticism.

The existence of leylines was first proposed by Watkins in his classic book "The Old Straight Track" published in 1925. He first noted the apparent linear alignment of ancient monuments such as churches, tumuli and standing stones by the casual use of a ruler on an Ordnance Survey map and this prompted him to make a more detailed study of these. He suggested that these alignments were the result of early farmers and tribesmen making surveys of the landscape, and marking sites, such as hill tops with a clear line of sight, with marker stones. These later may have resulted in the foundation of religious sites at these points, later still possibly becoming sites for churches.

During the last 30 years interest in leylines has intensified, and some people have linked them to UFO's, lines of force, astronomical and astrological alignments. Not surprisingly, this rather tended to give leylines a bad name rendering them unworthy of serious study. Hence an initial reluctance by some in our group to spend too much time studying this aspect of Thriplow!

Three alignments were investigated, initially as a result of joining up churches, ancient sites and hilltops as straight lines on the Landranger OS Map 154. Line1 (see chart) passes SE to NW through Thriplow Church stretching from Newport in the south to Hardwick in the north. A second line (line 2) is nearly 90 degrees to this, going SW to NE. The third alignment (line 3), while not passing through Thriplow, was sufficiently close to merit some investigation. This was the line connecting the churches of Therfield in the west, passing through Barley, Gt Chishall and Elmdon. This continued close to Strethall Church but not sufficiently close to be considered on-line.

Attempting to draw straight lines through all these sites resulted in a number of quite convincing alignments, but one or more of the sites were often some 100 m off line, depending on how the line was drawn, and who drew it! Since the resulting map alignments thus had a degree of uncertainty, the positions of these various points were checked with a Global Positioning System. This is a mobile phone sized gizmo capable of fixing its position on any point on the earth's surface (provided that it has a good view of the sky) utilizing signals from several satellites giving an accuracy of +/- 10 metres, at least 10x more precise than is possible with an OS map.

The GPS measurements at the church sites were taken at both the east and west ends and the average taken for the mid point.

When linear regression was performed on these points, the correlation coefficients all gave an astonishing 0.99, where 1.00 is an exact straight line. The equations are given in the plot opposite.

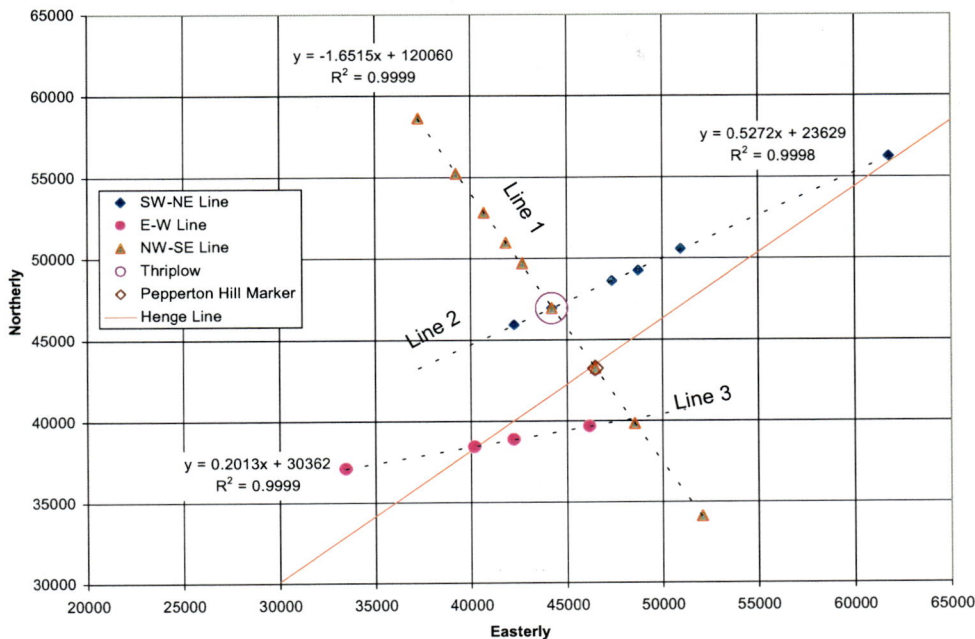

Chart showing four alignment lines plotted on Easterly (x-axis, 20000–65000) vs Northerly (y-axis, 30000–65000) grid.

Legend:
- SW-NE Line
- E-W Line
- NW-SE Line
- Thriplow
- Pepperton Hill Marker
- Henge Line

Equations on chart:
$y = -1.6515x + 120060$
$R^2 = 0.9999$

$y = 0.5272x + 23629$
$R^2 = 0.9998$

$y = 0.2013x + 30362$
$R^2 = 0.9999$

Line 1, Line 2, Line 3 labels

NW-SE Line 1
Hardwick
Harston
Lords Bridge footpath
on the N side of
Haslingfield
Rowleys Hill
Thriplow
Pepperton Marker
Strethall Church
Newport Church

SW-NE Line 2
(Melbourn Long
Barrow)
Fowlmere
Thriplow
Whittlesford
Sawston
Babraham
(Fleam Dyke gap)
Westley Waterless

E-W Line 3
Elmdon
Gt Chishall
Barley
Therfield

Line 1, starting form Newport Church, passes through Strethall Church and then across the top of the unnamed hill 1.5 miles to the NW. On this hill top, what appears to be an Iron Age hill fort has been identified from an aerial photograph. Further on the line passes over the top of the Pepperton Hill ridge which again exhibits some interesting crop marks. Intriguingly, very close to where the line crosses the Pepperton Hill ridge a rectangular block was found, about 35 x 19 x 12 cm, probably weighing around 25Kg. Could this have been one of the marker stones described by Watkins? The line then passes through Thriplow Church then passes just south of the trig point on Rowleys Hill and on to Harston Church. The line continues to the NE of Haslingfield, across a 90 degree bend in a footpath, and continues directly towards one of the radio telescope dishes (this IS regarded as coincidental!). It then crosses the A 603 at the point where the Bourn Brook passes underneath, but also where the footpath intersects the road. It then passes by the eastern end of the Foxes Bridge track at the point this turns south, ¾ mile to the south of Comberton. The final point we investigated on this alignment was Hardwick Church.

Line 2 (unlike Line1) has been the subject of previous study and follows the Icknield Way, passing through the villages of Fowlmere, Thriplow, Whittlesford, Sawston, Babraham and Westley Waterless. Of particular interest is the gap in Fleam Dyke approximately 1m SE of where it crosses the A11. If extended further to the NE it appears to pass very close to the southern extremity of Devils Dyke near to Stetchworth.

Line 3, from Therfield to Elmdon, since this only comprises 4 sites, would appear somewhat less convincing than the other two even though it does score a remarkable correlation coefficient of 0.9999.

Yet another intriguing alignment which the TLRG want to investigate more fully is between Stonehenge and what was believed to be a wooden henge at Arminghall, 1 m south of Norwich. Thriplow appears to be just about 2m to the north of this line which passes along the ridge of Pepperton Hill, (also on Line1 described above). This alignment is approximately 2 miles to the south of Line 1 at Thriplow, but converging with it and crossing it near Westley Waterless.

Grid Data from GPS measurements

Note: GPS data is can only be considered accurate to ± 10m unless particularly sophisticated equipment is used.

No attempt is being made, at present, to interpret these alignments, other than to comment that these appear to be too precisely in line to be coincidental. It perhaps helps to add weight to Francis Pryor's views that the Pre–Roman Britons were far from being the woad covered savages which is still sometimes imagined!

GRID DATA FROM GPS MEASUREMENTS

Note: GPS data is can only be considered accurate to ± 10m unless particularly sophisticated equipment is utilised.

Location	East	North	Distance from line
NW- SE (29 km) (Line 1)			metres
Hardwick	37234	58612	34
Lords Bridge	39226	55229	17
Haslingfield footpath	40696	52831	3
Harston	41824	50973	2
Rowleys Hill	42684	49717	82
Thriplow	44207	46957	48
Pepperton	46507	43240	8
Strethall	48552	39845	20
Newport	52067	34118	16
SW- NE (22 km) (Line 2)			
Fowlmere	42247	45931	27
Thriplow	44207	46957	20
Whittlesford	47373	48591	11
Sawston	48761	49240	84
Babraham	50971	50540	35
Westley Waterless	61802	56224	13
WSW- ENE (13 km) (Line 3)			
Elmdon	46183	39662	4
Gt Chishall	42216	38865	6
Barley	40164	38431	15
Therfield	33445	37099	5

THE USE OF COMPUTERS

When our project first got underway one of our group might have been described as a computer-phile, one a computer-phobe and the remainder in between. Almost all of us had access to a computer and we rapidly discovered the advantages of email as a means of sharing both text and images, and making meeting arrangements or discussing points. That is not to say this came easily, there were problems with the size and type of files, there were problems with different versions of word processing software. There were problems with virtually everything, but we solved them all sufficiently for our needs. Some even attended a training course on building a web site and did so! (www.thriplowlandscape. cambscommunitygroups.org.uk)

One of the most difficult problems we encountered was superimposing one image on another, such as resistivity results on a site survey or a site survey on an aerial photograph.

Plotting a site survey with a plane table has the advantage that it is easy to correct mistakes and the results unfold before your eyes. Unfortunately when you want to combine it with other data or images, you have the choice of working with lots of tracing paper or scanning your images into a computer first.

Scanning is no problem these days, but superimposing your scan on either a map, another survey, or a resistivity plot does present difficulties. The foremost of these is orientation, closely followed by scale and transparency. All of these may be overcome with standard image processing packages such as PaintShop Pro but can be very time consuming to achieve a good fit. More versatile programmes such as MapMaker Gratis (www. mapmaker.com which as the name implies is free), or TNT lite from MicroImages are designed for working with map based images and defined scales. The free versions of these two programmes do have limitations,

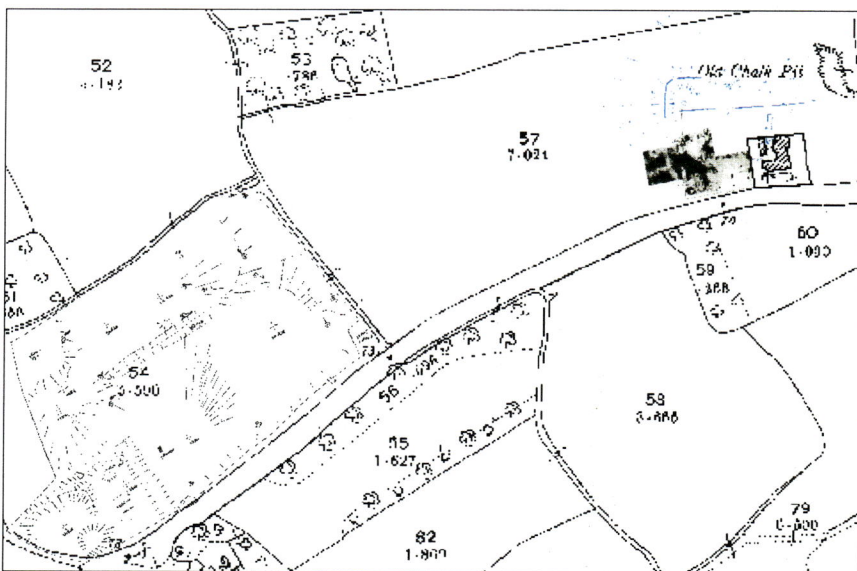

Superimposition of two plane table field surveys and some resistivity data on an old map.

the first of functionality, the second of project size. Most of our image processing has been done using MapMaker Pro, which allows survey images to be superimposed on aerial photographs and individual locations of finds to be plotted on scaled maps or surveys.

One major problem with a scanned image is line thickness. This is fixed at the time of the scan and any zooming in with an image processing programme results in a blurred or block definition of the image. If, on the other hand, a survey consists of a series of coordinates where a point of interest is x metres away on a bearing of y degrees, the data may be processed digitally. Some thought about Pythagorus' Theorum and a spreadsheet such as Excel makes converting distances and bearings into standard x,y or Eastings and Northings relatively straightforward. Digital processing using defined points has the advantage of maintaining its definition when the image is 'zoomed' because a line is drawn between the points – all of which are theoretically of zero thickness. If you want to explore this in more detail you will need to look up 'raster' and 'vector' graphics!

For straightforward plots of survey data points, eg how far away and in which direction, CogoCad from CMT (www.cmtinc.com) is free and quite versatile. It allows the input of data as distances and bearings or as x,y coordinates. The suppliers also provide a useful

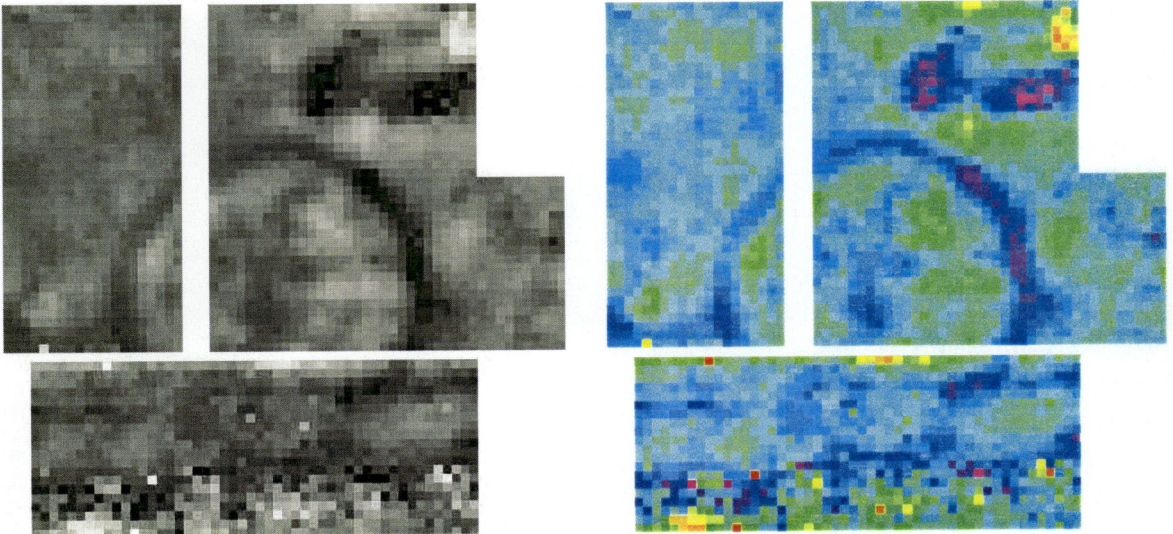

Resistivity plots from the tumulus in Thriplow, the same data processed in different ways.

programme (Contour) to create 3D images or contour plots from an X,Y,Z text file.

One of the best programmes we have used for creative processing of resistivity data is 'Snuffler' (http://www2.prestel.co.uk/aspen/sussex/snuffler.html). It is often difficult to identify meaningful patterns or shapes within raw resistivity images. This programme allows the same data to be presented in various colour scales as well as the usual grey scale, complete with options to remove spurious data and interpolate amongst many others.

Resign yourself to a learning curve in image processing. The results are well worth the effort both in constructing clear understandable pictures for presentation and for accurate location of archaeological sites. In the latter case, on one occasion we noticed a crop mark in one of multimaps' aerial photographs (www.multimap.com) and superimposed survey images from the Multi Agency Geographical Information System (www.magic.gov.uk), then carried out a resistivity survey based on the map measurements that was within 2-3m in a field with the nearest locatable feature over 150m away.

Survey plots from theodolite readings with colouring to show damp areas and ditch base plus resistivity.

OTHER PROGRAMMES.

It didn't take us too long to realise the value of word processors for writing notes and text. Most, but not all of us, used Microsoft Word or Works of various versions, and apart from having to download the odd converter programme from the Microsoft site we had few problems. For adding margin notes as you are going along though, you can't beat a paper and pencil! When we started looking at leylines we used Microsoft Excel - mainly because it was in the packages we had available. There are other programmes that would have offered more facilities for incorporating pictures with graphs, for example, but that would have meant spending money!

WRITING A BOOK

Microsoft again comes to the fore with Publisher - again mainly because we had it available. This caused us some problems to start with because of the total incompatibility between versions. In the end we solved this by one of our group agreeing to compile the book, whilst everyone else provided data in forms that could be cut and pasted into place.

The next paragraph is a bit technical, but has been left in because it might be a vital clue to someone in the future!

This produced immense frustration from time to time as we discovered interesting foibles such as limits on image file sizes - the jpeg file of 100kb that couldn't be inserted with no understandable reason why not, until you delve into the very small print that says there is a size limit, but with this type of file it is the uncompressed size that counts, not its given size.

The 'learning curve' with Publisher is not too bad but it is still there even if you have become comfortable with word processors. The biggest we experienced related to the overflowing text boxes and linking images and captions together.

Overall, we found it was helpful to have someone on the team who had expertise in computing, but that we could get there eventually under our own steam!

Postscript.

Having written the text, drawn or produced the pictures, and brought the parts for this book together, we discovered yet more problems to be overcome. These largely related to MS Publisher, which, although it has several features suggesting that it is capable of producing a file which is ready for printing by a 'commercial printer', in our experience this was not achievable.

Problem 1: Size.

This book as Publisher files is about 450Mb. This meant that to avoid it taking forever to get to a specific place, we had to split it into separate files for each trail, but even then the only way we could pass it between ourselves to discuss layouts was by means of a CD. Email was precluded by the size of files our service providers allowed to be transferred.

Problem 2: Pages.

In a book with a map spread over two pages, it would be silly to end up with the intended right hand page printed on the back of the intended left hand page. To achieve the correct layout we ended up with a blank page at the start of each section with no way of removing it and maintaining the correct layout.

Problem 3: Printers.

In our experience most small scale printers do not use Publisher and are wary of the printer files it produced ('postscript'). They were happier with 'pdf' files. We solved this problem using an Adobe programme, Acrobat; which also allowed us to combine Publisher files and remove the blank pages. This was looking promising until we found a printer that understood our problems who said we ought to print some test pages before going much further. What a sensible suggestion! We immediately discovered that black when printed on a colour page wasn't black, but a kind of yellow-grey. Ah ha said our printer - CMYK problem. Helpfully he explained that printers use Cyan Magenta Yellow and black and our document was in RGB (Red, Green and Blue) which is intended for viewing on a monitor screen. Back to Publisher and, delving in its depths, you can change this facet. Even after this correction though, matching grey shading proved challenging, and required manual alteration of the shading level on our boxes.

The basic conclusion we came to is that Publisher was not a good choice for a book, and that finding an understanding and helpful printer was a real benefit. (The printer in question has his details at the back!)

GEOLOGY OF THE THRIPLOW AREA

OVERVIEW

Thriplow is situated on low Chalk hills which run in a SW/NE direction. There is gentle relief with a local highpoint in the village at the church, and the land to the north of the village slopes gradually down to the Cam valley. To the south of Thriplow there is a broad shallow valley with an escarpment visible beyond.

The geology of Thriplow has created favourable conditions for people to settle: in particular, springs in the centre of the village and well drained, fertile chalky soils which are suitable for agriculture. Once cleared of woodland, the Chalk hills became an ancient routeway across the country with the high point a vantage point. There are useful resources within the parish – flints in the soil for tool making and building, a band of hard chalk called clunch, and also areas of woodland and gravel.

The diagrams in Trail 3, where the map is based on the Saffron Walden (Sheet 205) geological map, illustrate the geology of Thriplow. Most noticeable is the line of sites along the chalk hills where springs issue at Fowlmere, Thriplow, Chronicle Hills and beyond. These springs feed streams which flow north towards the River Rhee, a tributary of the River Cam.

How geological processes produced the present landforms can be summarised as follows. The underlying Chalk was laid down within the Cretaceous Period (135 – 65 million years ago). Subsequent rock layers have been eroded away leaving the Chalk as the present bedrock. About fifteen to twenty million years ago, the rock strata were tilted slightly to the SE. The softer Chalk beds eroded more quickly than the harder Chalk forming a gently undulating escarpment landscape, as shown in the cross-sectional diagram in

Trail 3.

The Ice Ages of the last two million years brought further changes. The ice sheets of the Anglian glaciation advanced over the area, and their retreat dumped large quantities of glacial material including boulder clay (also known as till), gravel and erratic boulders. This material has subsequently been redistributed by various processes, including by floods during thaws.

In the Devensian glaciation (or Last Ice Age), ice sheets reached the North Norfolk coast, and this area was in the grip of severe periglacial conditions with permafrost affecting the ground. These periglacial conditions led to a variety of landforms affecting a swathe of land running SW/NE across East Anglia. These landforms have some interesting names – for example, ice wedges, thermokarst, thaw lakes, palsas and pingos. They have left their mark on the landscape in a variety of ways, such as patterned or hummocky ground, convolutions in the soil and depressions sometimes filled by ponds. Hummocky ground and fossil pingos are found in Thriplow, and the area could even be the site of a thermokarst thaw lake. Some of these features may be a little over 10,000 years old, a blink of an eye in geological time!

THE CHALK

The chalk was laid down in horizontal beds about 100 to 70 million years ago in the Cretaceous Period, during times when East Anglia was submerged at least 200 metres below the sea. There are three main layers of chalk, known as Lower Chalk, Middle Chalk, and Upper Chalk with bands of harder fissured rock between them: Totternhoe Stone or Burwell Rock within the Lower Chalk, Melbourn Rock between the Lower and Middle Chalk, and Chalk Rock between the

Middle and Upper Chalk.

The rock layers have subsequently been tilted towards the Southeast and much eroded, so that now Lower Chalk (darker green on the map) forms the lower ground to the North and West, and the Middle Chalk (mid-green on the map in Trail 3) forms the higher ground in the Southeast of the parish. The hard bands of chalk, Melbourn Rock and Chalk Rock, are shown in dark green. Being slightly more resistant to erosion, they form the high point in Thriplow and the escarpment visible to the south, as shown in the diagrammatic cross-section in Trail 3.

The Lower and Middle Chalk are not particularly hard, except for the Totternhoe Stone. The Lower Chalk has two main divisions – the Chalk Marl below the Totternhoe Stone and the Grey Chalk above. The Lower Chalk contains no flints. The Chalk Marl (about 25 metres thick) is a soft greyish marl, which contains a lot of clay. The Totternhoe Stone layer is about 7 metres thick and is a lightish brown grey chalk with green coated nodules at its base. The Grey Chalk is about 23 metres thick. It is ordinary grey chalk in its lower part, but the upper part is distinctly white and is tough and blocky with irregular jointing. The Middle Chalk is greyish white and largely composed of nodular and lumpy marl-seamed chalk with only a few scattered flints except near the top.

The Melbourn Rock is a hard, yellowish, rocky Chalk full of small nodules and is two to three metres thick. In this part of Cambridgeshire, a local Chalk hard enough to be used in buildings is termed clunch. In Thriplow, clunch is Melbourn Rock and it was used as a low quality building material, for example in walls and floors, but it had to be protected from the rain. Clunch was excavated from the clunch pits in Thriplow. Those near the school and at the southern end of Middle Street are easily visible from the road. Beneath the Melbourn Rock is a thin layer of belemnite marls, up to a metre thick. In the past, it was thought that the Melbourn Rock and belemnite marls formed an impervious layer that caused the springs in Thriplow. However it is now thought that the belemnite marls bed may be too thin to be an important springline and that the springs arise mostly because of the impermeability of the Chalk Marl below the Totternhoe Stone.

The Upper Chalk contains flints. Though all the Upper Chalk has been eroded away at Thriplow, the hard flints resist erosion and many are found in the soil. They were a useful resource for earlier inhabitants of Thriplow for tool making or for building walls.

Many of these divisions of the Chalk have been superseded in recent times by formal lithostratigraphic units, which for the curious are described in 'Geology of the Saffron Walden district' by Moorlock et al. (2003).

The 70 million years between the deposition of the Chalk and the Ice Ages in the Quaternary Period (beginning about two million years ago) has left little trace on the present geology of the area except for the tilting of the rock layers to the southeast about fifteen to twenty million years ago.

THE ICE AGES

In the last two million years there have been many cycles of spreading and retreating ice sheets over Britain, and each has massively reshaped the landscape by erosion and subsequent deposition of material. The last time Thriplow was covered by an ice sheet was about 450,000 years ago during the Anglian Glaciation when the ice extended to a few miles north of London. In the last 500,000 years the climate has mostly been extremely cold. Roughly 100,000 year spells of intense cold have been interspersed with roughly 10,000 year intervals of warming. The last cold period named the Devensian occurred between about 100,000 to 10,000 years ago. We are at present in a 'warm' interval (known as the Flandrian or Holocene) that began about 10,000 years ago.

Glaciers have deposited boulder clay (also known as till), gravels and erratics (boulders and rocks) over the area. Rock material from the Highlands of Scotland, southern Scotland and Yorkshire are among those recognised. The present distribution of the glacial till partly results from it being moved around by various processes following deposition. During thaws, huge quantities of meltwater containing silt were released, and with the underlying ground still frozen and thus impermeable, the meltwater caused tumultuous flash floods, scouring out a new river course and re-depositing the debris carried within it. Such chaotic processes mean it can be very difficult today to look at the distribution of glacial till and confidently say how and where it was laid down.

There are large areas of gravel in the southern part of Thriplow parish. In 1881, they were thought to have been deposited by a series of ancient streams, but on the geological map of 1938 they are designated as Taele Gravels. (During the Ice Ages, gravel near the surface in frozen sloping ground will gradually slip down slope if the surface is periodically warmed and melted by the sun's radiation. This process is known as solifluction. The accumulation of such gravel at the bottom of a slope in this area is termed Taele Gravel). In this case, it is suggested that the gravels have moved down slope from the high escarpment to the south.

A recent theory favours the 'ancient river system' idea of 1881. This theory suggests that there was an ancient river flowing roughly on the alignment of the A505, from Wardington Bottom just east of Royston and joining the River Cam somewhere near Whittlesford. This is thought to have been in existence after the Anglian Glaciation, and perhaps before.

The stream carried so much debris it formed a braided river plain and laid down large areas of gravel. The gravel areas tend to protect the ground beneath them from the scouring action of the river, which in time formed new lower courses and deposited gravels at those lower levels. In this way, several gravel spreads at different levels were deposited.

At some time in the Devensian, a minor stream began to flow along the present River Rhee alignment. It may be that as the headwaters of the Rhee cut back its valley, and the springs at Wardington Bottom began to dry up, the Rhee 'captured' the water flowing eastward near Flint Cross, diverting it west of Fowlmere to Shepreth and into the River Cam.

PERIGLACIAL EFFECTS

During the intensely cold but unglaciated times, Thriplow suffered severe periglacial conditions with permafrost up to 16 metres deep affecting the ground. Along a SW/NE swathe of East Anglia, at the end of the Devensian, conditions were suitable for periglacial land features to be produced. Their remnants are visible today because there has been no major erosional event since. Periglacial landforms include patterned and hummocky ground, thermokarst depressions and thaw lakes, pingos, ice wedges and contortions in the sediments near the surface.

Many periglacial effects occur because although the term 'permafrost' conjures up a landscape frozen and unalterable, the surface of the frozen ground will periodically be melted by the sun's radiation. The top layer, known as the active layer, therefore goes through many cycles of freezing and thawing. The material within the active layer is sorted and moved around. Eventually, the ground may look hummocky, as in the centre of Thriplow, or patterned with polygonal cells or stripes– one example occurs at Elvedon in Suffolk. When a vertical section of the ground can be examined, for example at Great Shelford, the convolutions in the sediments can be seen in the riverbank. Augering of the ground in Thriplow Meadows has shown a similar mixing of the sediments.

There are other periglacial features locally including thermokarst hollows and pingos. Irregular depressions produced by the melting of ground ice are termed thermokarst. Angela Taylor has made detailed investigations of thermokarst depressions in Whittlesford. In Thriplow, the remnants of pingos are evident and it may even be possible that the village is the site of an ancient thermokarst thaw lake.

The pingos at Thriplow are the open-system type, occuring because of the springs. The groundwater table within the chalk roughly follows the relief. Fissures in the Totternhoe Stone make it permeable and groundwater can flow within it. However, the high clay content in the Chalk Marl beneath makes an impermeable barrier. The groundwater in the Totternhoe Stone is under pressure due to the high water table in the hills to the South – the pressure of perhaps 45 metres of water causes the springs to rise.

In permafrost conditions, a spring will form a lens of ice near the ground surface, and continue to feed it, enlarging it and pushing up the ground surface, see the diagram in Trail 4. The freezing and thawing of its soil covering layer will cause the material to slip down the sides of the pingo, forming a ring of debris around it. Eventually, the covering layer will be breached and

the ice lens will melt, leaving a circular depression surrounded by a rampart. Where the spring persists, a pond may form in the depression. A good place to see pingo depressions is Walton Common in Norfolk.

A thaw lake in a periglacial landscape is a shallow, usually roughly circular lake. It is thought to originate as a small pond which does not completely refreeze in winter. It can enlarge quite rapidly. The frozen ground around its edges is melted by the warmer water in the pond and slips downwards. In the case of pingo ponds in chalk areas, the solubility of the chalk speeds the process. In this way, a shallow, flat bottomed, roughly circular thaw lake can be formed, often bounded by more resistant rocks.

If the thaw lake edges are breached, for example by headward erosion of a stream, the lake is drained and a shallow, flat bottomed, roughly circular depression containing silt from the eroded rocks is left.

Such landforms have been recognised in Cambridgeshire e.g. at Grunty Fen. It has been suggested that the flat area in Thriplow which is almost encircled by the Melbourn Rock outcrop could have been formed in a similar manner, when a thaw lake developed from a spring fed pingo pond, and later drained northwards.
It is remarkable that these periglacial landscape features at Thriplow were formed perhaps only twenty to ten thousand years ago.

We thank Dr Steve Boreham for his help with this section.

GLOSSARY

A

Anglo-Saxons - these peoples ended up living in our islands having emigrated from what is now North Germany and Denmark. They caught the ferry in about 400AD just as the Romans were going the other way. It is thought that they were a rather lumpen people who did not change very much in the 700 years that they were in charge of the place. However, they did a lot of farming and were not too fond of town living.

Animal remains - you can learn a lot about how our ancestors lived by looking for the remains of the animals they had for lunch. Just as well they were not vegetarians.

Animals - domestic animals can be a pain in the butt for archaeologists who need to survey or dig up the field where they are living. It is usual to have to contend with stampeding cows, randy horses and very hungry goats- so beware.

Archaeology - this subject covers a multitude of activities relating to our past from say the study of Egyptian Pyramids (in rather short supply in Cambridgeshire) to trying to recreate Stone Age living conditions. The more civilised end of the subject is Landscape Archaeology where you can sit at home and look at maps all day. (See separate entry)

Artefacts - these are the things that get dug up from archaeological digs. They are the Holy Grail to archaeologists as without them there would be nothing to write about or exhibit in museums.

Aerial Photography – if you are a rich archaeologist then you should have your own aeroplane – not to whiz off on holiday in but to take photographs of all those exciting humps and bumps seen from the air in the fields below you. Exploring in this way by air came into its own after 1945 when our local area was surveyed by J.K.St Joseph from Cambridge University and now the University holds an amazing collection of photographs of the UK and beyond.

Auger - if you are fit a spot of auguring will put you in good heart! It involves screwing a hollow rod into the soil so that a sample from several metres down can be extracted and analysed. This will give information on the underlying soil as it can be examined to see if pollen from various sources is present. This in turn will help determine what the growing conditions were like several hundred years ago. Archaeologists can then decide whether the area was covered in trees, grassland or under water and so form a view as to what was happening at the time.

B

Barrow - this is not something off a building site but a word used by archaeologists to describe a burial mound. Its origin is from the German word *berg*, meaning a hill. There are several in this part of Cambridgeshire. (see also tumuli)

Beer - a vital drink to people throughout the ages as the fermentation process purified the water. Still used by archaeologists to this day.

Benchmark - this is a sign that the people from the Ordnance Survey scattered around the countryside marking heights above sea level. The design is in the form of a rudimentary picnic bench – hence the name. There are clear marks to be seen on the Thriplow church tower and on the school building. However, many that are marked on maps are not always easy to find!

Black Death - this is the rather macabre name given to an outbreak of bubonic plague that took hold in England during the middle of the 14th century. Some estimates show that half the population died and a clear indication of this can be seen in the list of priests often shown in Parish churches. During this time the turnover in incumbents rose dramatically with often two priests or more per year being appointed.

Bronze Age - this is a general description of the time between 2500 and 800 BC when bronze, an alloy of tin and copper, was used as the preferred metal for cooking in and also for bashing each other on the head with axes. It always was a rare and hence expensive item so not too many people living then had the chance to parade around in suits of bronze armour.

Burials - it is just as well that our ancestors made a big deal out of giving their relations a good send off when they died, as most archaeological sites are burials or cremations. Odd to think that many an archaeologists career has been made out of a pile of old bones.

C

Clunch – if you are faced with wanting to build a house in an area without any natural stone, as in South Cambridgeshire, the answer lies underfoot. There is plenty of chalk available near the surface and so lumps of it were dug out, roughly shaped and used as building bricks. This is called clunch. People who still live in cottages made of clunch claim it is warm and cosy!

Carbon dating - what would archaeologists have done for dating objects without a physical chemist coming to their aid? In 1960 Prof. Libby received the Nobel Prize in chemistry for developing the technique in which organic materials can be fairly well dated up to 40,000 years ago. It is now standard for archaeologists to ask a laboratory to date objects that they have found (if they can afford it)

Celts - these are the peoples that inhabited these islands before the Romans turned up. They seemed to scare the living daylights out of the Romans to begin with as they had the habit of painting themselves all over with a blue dye derived from the woad plant- or at least so the legend goes! It seems more likely that they were just cold. It is thought that there are still real live Celts living in our midst today in the guise of the Welsh and Scots.

Countryside Agency - this is a statutory body set up in 1999 firstly to conserve and enhance the natural beauty of the countryside, secondly to promote social equity and economic opportunity for the people who live there, and thirdly to help everyone to enjoy this national asset. It is also the body that oversees the working of the Local Heritage Initiative. (which see).

Crop Marks - Archaeologists pray for dry weather conditions when crops are growing in fields that may have interesting features to reveal. This is because plants will grow at different rates when the underlying soil covers walls or ditches and so patterns appear that outline the below ground features. An aeroplane is a useful accessory as flying over the fields saves a great deal of climbing church towers to peer over adjacent fields. A setting sun or snow lying on fields will sometimes cast the right shadow to show up hidden humps and bumps. However, a rising sun never seems so popular with archaeologists.

D

Dark Ages - this nocturnal phrase is often used by archaeologists to describe the time after the Romans packed their bags and left and the coming of the Normans in the famous year 1066. The reason it is so dark is that no one seems to know what was happening. Not much change then.

Dendrochronology - this is the technical word that describes tree ring dating. As some trees are very long lived it was thought that a study of the pattern of growth rings (one added per year) when the tree was felled would give a way of dating- a subject dear to an archaeologist's heart. In practice it works quite well but is limited by the size and completeness of the sample and will only date the last 5000 years or so. Also counting tree rings all day is much like counting sheep at night.

Deserted Villages - the idea that some parts of our present day open countryside once had thriving village communities which are now lost is an important part of Landscape archaeology. After the Black Death (see entry) the population was not sufficient to fill all the villages and so many of the more marginal communities went to the wall. The remains of the village streets and house foundations can sometimes be seen as humps and bumps in the fields. A good example of one such site is at Clopton, near to Wimpole estate in Cambridgeshire. In the trade these sites are often abbreviated to DMV or Deserted Mediaeval Villages.

Dowsing - some people claim to have the ability to see what is hidden below ground by walking over the field clutching either metal or wooden sticks in their hands. Now this must be of interest to archaeologists as they spend a fair part of their lives wondering what is under the ground they are walking on. However, experiments show that the effects recorded by dowsers are by and large not reproducible so its back to the hard slog of finding our heritage by other means.

E

Excavation - this is a technical term used by archaeologists to describe digging large holes in the ground in the hope of finding something interesting on the way down.

F

Field systems - this is a phrase used by landscape archaeologists to describe what farmers have been up to in the past. Due to the grave lack of chemical know-how by our ancestors they had to rotate the crops sown in their fields to preserve any hope of keeping the ground fertile. This usually meant taking one field out of use per growing season for it to recover its store of minerals. Detailed knowledge of the fields surrounding a village gives clues to the way farming was practised in the past.

Field walking - this is a great way to get your friends and relations involved in archaeology. All you need is a farmer who is willing to have people tramp over a field, say 10 people (any number can join in) and a large wad of plastic bags. The idea is that each person walks in a straight line down the field with his next door neighbour 2 metres away. Every 2 metres the line stops and everybody looks for interesting items on the ground. These are put into the plastic bags and marked up accordingly. The process is repeated until the end of the field is reached or it's time for the pub to open. The finds can be analysed comfortably later. The serious point about field walking is that the concentration of say pottery shards found is in proportion to the size and age of the community that may have been living nearby.

Flints - Archaeologists like flints! Mostly because an ancient worked flint looks identical to one made last week so it's possible to construct stories around finding flints without much fear of contradiction. However, a true specimen is a wonderful thing to see as it represents man's first steps in creating a modern controlled environment.

G

GPS- Global Positioning System - this satellite navigation system has been developed especially for archaeologists who are notorious for not knowing exactly where they are. However, as the accuracy is at best 10 meters or so it is not recommended for working near to cliff edges in the dark.

Ground penetrating radar - the latest toy for archaeologists who fancy themselves as technological wizards. The equipment looks much like a cheap electric lawnmower and is pushed over the ground that is under investigation. The results though can be quite dramatic, as it is capable of producing a 3 dimensional image of the structure under the surface.

H

Hill forts - these structures were built by people living in the Iron Age (which see). We are fortunate that in South Cambridgeshire we have one of the best examples of a hill fort at Wandlebury. However, there are others to see and read about and ones that on first sight are not especially on top of a hill. The one in Sawston is in this category. Archaeologists are always on the look out for likely sites as it is the ambition of many to discover a new fort and so become almost famous.

Hoards - when the political situation was looking particularly nasty our ancestors often took the precaution of burying most of their worldly processions in their back garden. Sadly, it seems that some of the owners either forgot where they buried the loot or died before they had a chance to reclaim it. This turns out to be good news for archaeologists as if it can be identified then the resulting find is a time capsule from the time of the burial. Often the hoard is whisked off to the local museum for display or if it is something really special to the British Museum with lots of publicity.

I

Iron Age - believe it or not but there was once a time when lumps of iron were considered to be worth having. This was from about 800BC to 43AD (when the Romans turned up). The reason for this excitement about iron is that is much harder than bronze and so iron swords and axes could demolish those lower down the arms race. Iron ore is also more widely distributed than tin or copper ores and so ultimately iron objects came to dominate the way people lived.

L

Landscape Archaeology - this is a branch of archaeology that has come to the fore in the quest to find out how our ancestors lived. It is thought that there are clues left in the landscape that we see today that lead us to answers concerning where people lived, how they constructed their houses, how they traded and where their dead were buried. It can be an armchair activity armed only with a map and a good imagination - however true devotees will be out in all weathers peering at strange bumps in the landscape hoping to find a lost village or at least a moated manor site. A nice healthy outdoor occupation!

Leylines - those with a mystical frame of mind will be intrigued to read the landscape in terms of these nebulous straight lines that join ancient sites to one another. The idea was first mooted by a man called Alfred Watkins who wrote a book (The Old Straight Track) in which he put forward the view that the original tracks in Britain were aligned in some way. People who wished to put a mystical slant to the concept exploited these ideas.

It may be difficult for professional archaeologists to take this seriously but we have some results on the alignment of churches in Cambridgeshire that may need further explanation!

LHI - Local Heritage Initiative. This is the branch of the National Lottery that gives grants to local organisations, such as amateur archaeological societies. This has been a great benefit to those willing to make a commitment to the local community to explain how their village came into being.

Lithics - this is a posh name for stones!

M

Magnetometer surveys - we have all played with magnets and seen how they repel and attract one another. In fact the Earth is also a giant magnet and so if we use a very sensitive way of measuring the changes in the Earth's magnetic field we can see what may be causing them hidden under the ground. Archaeologists use this technique, as certain metallic objects will be shown up quite clearly. When the people on 'Time Team' call for a 'geophiz' survey then mostly likely this is what they will be doing! (See also Resistivity Surveys)

Maps – for a Landscape Archaeologist being without a map is unthinkable! Maps come in all shapes and sizes but to be of any use for study then the scale needs to be 1:25000 (or 4 cm on the map represents 1 km in real life). For investigating individual fields and houses then 10 cm to 1 km is recommended. There is also a fascination with old maps as there is the opportunity to see how the landscape has changed over the years; the problem with this is that the old map makers were sometimes rather liberal with the scale being used and also added rather fanciful descriptions at the request of the landowner at the time.

Medieval or Middle Ages - generally considered to range from AD 1200 to 1500. We are now at a time in history that is becoming recorded by the educated few in the country and so become the province of historians rather than archaeologists. Still lots to dig up and discover though!

Megalithic - literally translated as 'big stones'. What most people think of as Stonehenge will fit the description.

Metallurgy - the advances in technology that our ancestors achieved seemed to revolve around the better understanding of how to use metals. Has to be said that this was mostly driven by the need to bash one's neighbour over the head with a better axe. However, like our present day situation eventually the new metals became accepted as part of every day life hence the progression from stone to copper to bronze to iron.

Metal detecting - our ancestors left behind many metal objects and so a piece of kit that will pinpoint their whereabouts underground has been seized on by treasure hunters. The equipment was first developed to find mines in wartime and is now widely available and relatively cheap to buy. Treasure hunters have had a bad press as they often disrupt the archaeological site and are generally quite secretive as to where the objects they have found have come from. However, there is now a much better understanding between reputable metal detectorists and archaeologists, which is benefiting the study of our heritage.

Moats - these features in the landscape are not the magnificent areas of water surrounding castles that might be imagined but are the remains of ditches that were filled with water in the Middle Ages (which see). They are often found surrounding a raised platform where a house would have stood. There is a slight puzzle as to why all the effort and cost was put into digging these ditches but the view from archaeologists is that they represent a very fine status symbol. What could be better to show off to your neighbours a house with moat attached? It also proved useful to keep fish in, to have an instant source of water to put out fires and a convenient way to dispose of all those domestic waste products that we nowadays flush away.

Museums - these institutions are stuffed with items that are not always on display. If you are at all interested in your local heritage take an afternoon off and visit your nearest museum. The staff will be very pleased to hear your request and will usually drag up items from the back room for you to see.

P

Place Names - a whole sub-section of archaeology has evolved that deals with the analysis of village and town names. A great deal can be found out about a village from its name, for example a Viking settlement is often a word ending in –by. What people will make of Milton Keynes in the future is open for discussion!

Pseudo-archaeology - people seem to have the need to believe in events that are not likely to have happened and in the study of archaeology there are many examples of this. The most obvious are the ideas that a continent was lost in prehistoric times (the Atlantis story) or that we are descended from ancient astronauts (the Chariots of the Gods story). Nearer to our time and place is the mystery of the 'Gods' that Dr. Lethbridge discovered set out in the chalk on the side of a hill at Wandlebury hill fort. All these stories are fascinating reading but must be taken with a large pinch of salt.

R

References - all academic disciplines that rely on a systematic collection of literature need to be able to look up past work held on file or in journals. Archaeology is no exception to this and before any explorations are started a search through the literature for references relating to the project should be made. If that sounds a bit dreary then try it on a wet Monday afternoon!

Rescue archaeology - as our countryside becomes covered with houses it is important to see if foundations are cutting through layers of archaeology. This is where rapid response teams of archaeologists swing into action before the bulldozers arrive. This has been a growth area as many archaeologists earn their living in this way, as it is the duty of the property developer to commission and pay for a study before any building can commence.

Ritual – a word much beloved by archaeologists especially when coupled with 'site'. Archaeologists are always puzzled by what our ancestors got up to between the odd bit of farming and a fight or two. The gap in our knowledge can be filled by the idea of everyone praying and slaughtering a few animals. To do this properly of course special 'ritual sites' are called for so any unexplained area investigated by archaeologists ends up by being so labelled. Our ancestors are probably having a quiet spin in their graves at the thought!

Romans in Britain (AD 43 to 410) - on the whole the Romans have a good press when they are being discussed. It is thought that they brought much needed central heating to the natives along with a liking for wine and olive oil, not to mention those long straight roads. However, not everyone agreed at the time, as the Romans were to find out from Boudicca - a local lady from Norfolk. Fortunately for archaeologists there are plenty of sites to investigate and write long discussions about for many years to come.

Roman Villas - the thought of all those toga clad Romans lounging on their sofas eating grapes held aloft by their slaves has made life in a Roman villa so interesting. However, fact may have been a bit less exciting but nevertheless the remains of villas excavated in Britain has shown wonderful mosaic floors and wall decorations. In South Cambridgeshire and North Essex there are a few sites to see the outlines of a villa, but you would need to travel to St Albans or Chichester (Fishbourne) to see proper excavated villas.

S

Scientific archaeology - the use of scientific methods in archaeology is mirrored by the upsurge in science in our lives. It is now possible to date artefacts, see what they are made of and possibly who made it, all from laboratory equipment. It is also possible to pinpoint archaeological sites by satellite and produce a 3D image of what may be lurking below the surface. However, some archaeologists feel that this misses out on important sociological considerations which all the gadgets in the scientists' arsenal will not help solve. This sort of discussion helps to keep the study of our heritage alive.

Stone Age - (11,000BC to 2500BC) our ancestors lived for a long period in time without the benefit of metal implements, using instead stone axes, flints and bones. The description of these times as cave men leading a brutal life may not be quite correct as some of the tools that have been discovered are very elegant. As they tended to move around in pursuit of game herds it is very difficult for archaeologists to identify any settlement in our part of Britain.

Stonehenge - the ultimate site in Britain for archaeologists. It makes them very happy to talk for hours on how and why it was put together.

Stratigraphy - this is archaeologist speak for the various layers in the earth.

Soil resistivity survey - this technique is used to find out hidden structures under ground. It is much used on the 'Time Team' TV programme as it gives very colourful pictures on charts to show to viewers who are mightily impressed.

Surveying - land surveying is an important part of an archaeological expedition as you need to know where you are digging, but as it tends to involve angles and sums not too many archaeologists are very good at it.

T

Tumuli - posh word for barrows (which see).

V

Vikings - these are the gentlemen who wore horned helmets and generally made a nuisance of themselves between the time the Saxons turned up and before the Normans (who were only partly reformed Vikings) landed in 1066.

W

Water courses - the plotting of where the water flows around a village can lead to a lot of information as to where the original settlement was situated.

LIST OF BOOKS FOR FURTHER READING

Roman Britain from the Air
S.S.Frere & J.St Joseph
Cambridge University Press 1983

The Making of the English Landscape
W.G.Hoskins
WBC 1955

Archaeology of Cambridgeshire Vols 1 & 2
A.Taylor Cambridgeshire
County Council 1998

History on the Ground
M. Beresford
Sutton Publishing 1998

Man Made the Landscape
A.Baker & J. Harley
David & Charles 1973

The Changing Face of Britain
E. Hyams
Paladin 1977

Follow the Map – the Ordnance Survey Guide
J. Wilson A.&C.
Black 1985

English Place Names
K. Cameron
Batsford 1996

The Roman Villa in Britain
Rivet
Routledge 1969

Town & Country in Roman Britain
Rivet
Hutchinson 1958

English Landscapes
W.G. Hoskins
BBC 1973

Historical Britain
E. Wood
Harvill 1995

Cambridgeshire from the Air
S. Oosthuizen
Sutton 1996

Signposts to the Past
M. Gelling
Dent 1978

Villages in the Landscape
T. Rowley
Dent 1978

The Bronze Age Round Barrow in Britain
P. Ashbee
Phoenix 1960

The History of the Countryside
O. Rackham
Dent 1986

Roads & Tracks of Britain
C. Taylor
Dent 1979

The Common Stream
R. Parker
Paladin 1974

The Decline & Fall of Roman Britain
N. Faulkner
Tempus 2000

Current Scientific Techniques in Archaeology
P. Parkes
Croom Helm 1986

Early Cambridgeshire
A. Taylor, D. Browne & H. Darby
Oleander Press 1978

Unravelling the Landscape
ed. Mark Bowden
Tempus 1999

An Atlas of Cambridgeshire and Huntingdonshire History
ed. Tony Kirby and Susan Oosthuizen
Centre for Regional Studies   Anglia Polytechnic University   2000

Fields in the English Landscape
Christopher Taylor
J M Dent & Sons   1975

Landscape Archaeology
Michael Aston and Trevor Rowley
David and Charles   1974

Fieldwork for Archaeologists and Local Historians
Anthony Brown
Batsford   1987

History on your Doorstep
J R Ravensdale
BBC   1982

The Making of English Towns
David W Lloyd
Victor Gollancz   1984, 1992

Shell Guide to Reading the Landscape
Richard Muir
Michael Joseph   1981

Climatic History in the Modern World
H.H.Lamb
Methuen   1982

Climates of the British Isles
A.Ogilvie and G.Farmer
Routledge   1992

Weird Weather
P.Simons
Little, Brown and Co.   1996

Roman Britain
H.H.Scullard
Thames and Hudson 1995

Geology of Saffron Walden District
B.S.P. Moorlock, S.Boreham, M.A.Woods and M.G. Sumbler
British Geological Survey. NERC 2003

British Regional Geology   East Anglia and Adjoining Areas
C P Chatwin
HMSO   1961

The Cambridge Region   1965
J A Steers (ed)
British Association for the Advancement of Science 1965

Natural Landscapes of Britain from the Air
Nicholas Stephens (ed)
CUP   1990

Revealing the Buried Past
Chris Gaffney and John Gater
Tempus   2004

About Thriplow
Peter Speak and Shirley Wittering
The Thriplow Society 1995

The Church of St. George and All Saints in Thriplow
G.O.Vinter 1951

INDEX

Cover, from the first Ordnance Survey map of the area, 1903.

Published by Thriplow Landscape Research Group, 71 Fowlmere Road, Heydon, Royston. SG8 8PZ

Printed by Ryecroft Data, Graphic House, High Street, Fowlmere, Royston, SG8 7SU
01763 208640
www.ryecroftdata.co.uk

ISBN 0-9548085-0-9

Local Heritage *initiative*

Heritage Lottery Fund

Nationwide

The Countryside Agency